The Romantic Tradition in American Literature

The Romantic Tradition in American Literature

Advisory Editor

HAROLD BLOOM
Professor of English, Yale University

EONCHS OF RUBY

A Gift of Love

T[HOMAS] H[OLLEY] CHIVERS

ARNO PRESS

A NEW YORK TIMES COMPANY

New York • 1972

Reprint Edition 1972 by Arno Press Inc.

The Romantic Tradition in American Literature
ISBN for complete set: 0-405-04620-0
See last pages of this volume for titles.

Manufactured in the United States of America

ᎧᏍᎧᏍᎧᏍᎧᏍᎧᏍᎧᏍᎧᏍᎧᏍ

Library of Congress Cataloging in Publication Data

Chivers, Thomas Holley, 1809-1858.
    Eonchs of ruby; a gift of love.

    (The Romantic tradition in American literature)
    I. Title. II. Series.
PS1294.C4E6 1972   811'.3   72-4957
ISBN 0-405-04629-4

EONCHS OF RUBY.

A Gift of Love.

BY T. H. CHIVERS, M. D.

"The precious music of the heart."—*Wordsworth.*

New-York:
PUBLISHED BY SPALDING & SHEPARD.

1851.

JOHN P. PRALL, *Printer*,
9 Spruce Street, New-York.

CONTENTS.

THE VIGIL IN AIDEN.

—

In the Rosy Bowers of Aiden,
With her ruby-lips love-laden,
Dwelt the mild, the modest Maiden
　　Whom Politian called Lenore.
As the churches, with their whiteness,
Clothe the earth, with her uprightness
Clothed she now his soul with brightness,
　　Breathing out her heart's love-lore ;
For her lily-limbs so tender,
Like the Moon in her own splendor,
Seemed all earthly things to render
　　Bright as Eden was of Yore.
As the Morning Moon, when stricken
By the God of Day, will sicken,
Withering quite as Day doth quicken—
　　Faded now the Moon Lenore !
For she said to him, when dying,
On the bed where she was lying,
Breathing out her soul in sighing,
　　" Kiss thy dying lost Lenore !"

1

Then he cried out broken-hearted,
In this desert-world deserted,
Though she had not yet departed—
   "Are we not to meet, dear Maiden!
    In the Rosy Bowers of AIDEN,
   As we did in Days of Yore?"
And that modest, mild, sweet Maiden,
In the Rosy Bowers of AIDEN,
With her lily-lips love-laden,
   Answered, "Yes! forever more!"
And the old-time Towers of Aiden
   Echoed, "Yes! forever more!"

II.

Round his neck her arm now placing,
Lovely Death with Life embracing,
Heavenly Death the earthly gracing—
   She to him her soul did pour—
"Love! remember our first meeting!
O! forget not this last greeting!
This request my soul repeating—
   Kiss thy dying lost LENORE!
Take this ring—it was the token
Of thy vows to me first spoken—
Let those vows remain unbroken,
   Locked within thy heart's deep core!
Should you ever love another,
Love her only as her brother—
Or as we shall one another
   When we meet on that bright shore!
From the Flowery Fields ELYSIAN
I will come to thee, POLITIAN!
In some heavenly midnight vision,
   As I did in Days of Yore!"

Then he cried out broken-hearted,
Though she had not yet departed,
In this desert-world deserted—
    " Are we not to meet, dear Maiden !
      In the Rosy Bowers of AIDEN,
    As we did in Days of Yore ?"
And that modest, mild, sweet Maiden,
In the Rosy Bowers of AIDEN,
With her lily-lips love-laden,
    Answered, " Yes ! forever more !"
And the old-time Towers of Aiden
    Echoed, " Yes ! forever more !"

III.

Oh ! the plaintive sweet beseeching
Of those lips that Death was bleaching,
All his inmost soul now reaching,
    Reaching into his heart's core !
Such as heavenly Joy might borrow
From her earthly sister SORROW,
Should she promise her to-morrow
    Joys as bright as those of Yore.
Then with his whole soul he kissed her—
As an Angel, or his sister—
And, in God's great name, he blest her,
    Weeping out his heart's deep gore !
Like the half-grown Moon declining,
Through the clouds around her shining,
On her dying bed reclining,
    Lay the Angel-Moon LENORE !
Then her mother cried, " *My Daughter* '"
As from earth the Angels caught her—
She had passed the Stygian water
    On the Asphodelian shore !

Then he cried out broken-hearted,
For the best beloved departed—
In this desert-world deserted—
   "Are we not to meet, dear Maiden !
    In the Rosy Bowers of AIDEN,
   As we did in days of Yore ?"
And the voice of that sweet Maiden,
From the Rosy Bowers of AIDEN,
As with deep grief overladen,
   Answered, " Never—never more !"
And the old-time Towers of Aiden
   Echoed, " Never—never more !"

IV.

Then, beside the silent river,
Where he wandered still forever,
By her lonely grave that ever
   Seemed to Heaven the only door—
Through the amethystine morning
Came foul Lucifer returning
Up from Hell, where he was burning—
   This Elysian chant to pour—
" When the world was crucifying
JESUS CHRIST, when he was dying,
Shaking Heaven with his loud crying,
   While his soul dropt tears of gore—
From the Flowery Fields ELYSIAN
Saints returned in deep derision—
Bursting graves to see the VISION,
   Such as none had seen before !
Hell itself grew broken-hearted—
Wailed aloud for the departed !
Even the sun now seemed deserted,
   From the sackcloth that he wore !

Then I cried out broken-hearted—
In this desert-world deserted—
Ever true to the DEPARTED—
   ' Are we not to meet, dear Maiden !
  In the Rosy Bowers of AIDEN,
  As we did in days of Yore ?'
And RELIGION, that sweet Maiden,
In the Rosy Bowers of AIDEN,
With her lily-lips love-laden,
   Answered, ' Never—never more !'
And the old-time Towers of Aiden
   Echoed, ' Never—never more !'

v.

" From his bright incarnate Temple
Earth's great iron hoof did trample
Back his soul to God, as sample
   Of the sin that grieved him sore !
When, all glorified, ascending,
Heaven to meet him now descending,
Flights of Angels on him tending,
   Shouting ' GOD !' as they did soar !
Those ambrosial TRUTHS revealing
Down the echoing stars high wheeling,
In empyreal thunders pealing,
   Crashing, crumbling on Time's shore !
Tearing Hell's dark throne asunder,
Filling all the world with wonder,
Underneath the crushing thunder
   Of his lightning-TRUTHS of Yore !
Flooding all the wide Creation
With their joyful Jubilation,
Poured in blissful evocation,
   Till the world was flooded o'er !

Then I cried out broken-hearted—
Ever true to the DEPARTED—
In this desert-world deserted—
 ' Are we not to meet, dear Maiden !
  In the Rosy Bowers of AIDEN,
 As we did in Days of Yore ?'
And RELIGION, that sweet Maiden,
In the Rosy Bowers of AIDEN,
With her lily-lips love-laden,
 Answered, ' Never—never more !'
And the old time Towers of Aiden
 Echoed, ' Never—never more !'

VI.

" Thus from Earth now agonizing,
In his sun-like chariot rising,
All the stars in Heaven surprising
 With eclipse as they did soar—
Now like Paradise-Islands gleaming,
In the far-off ether beaming,
Floods of glory on them streaming
 Down from Heaven's eternal shore—
To that God-built City blazing,
Rapturous thundershouts upraising,
Pouring out their souls, in praising,
 To the God they did adore—
While each glorified Immortal
Thronged the blazing golden Portal—
Filling Salem's great high court all,
 There to meet their LORD once more—
On the wings of Angels soaring,
Rose the God they were adoring,
To his Father him restoring,
 Where he sat enthroned before !

Then I cried out broken-hearted—
Ever true to the DEPARTED—
In this desert-world deserted—
   ' Are we not to meet, dear Maiden !
    In the Rosy Bowers of AIDEN,
   As we did in Days of Yore ?'
And RELIGION, that sweet Maiden,
In the Rosy Bowers of AIDEN,
   With her lily-lips love-laden,
Answered, ' Never—never more !'
And the old-time Towers of Aiden
   Echoed, ' Never—never more !' "

VII.

Then, beside the silent river,
Where he waited still forever,
By her lonely grave that ever
   Seemed to Heaven the only door—
A white SWAN, all heavenly-gifted,
Like to living snow uplifted,
On her saintly pinions drifted,
   Came her dying song to pour !
Like the crescent moon sedately,
On some cloudless night, all stately,
Or, as on her couch lay lately
   The incarnate Moon LENORE—
Breathing out her soul in silence
For the Heaven-uplifted Highlands
Of the floating argent Islands
   Sailing now her soul before—
Floated now this argent NAID,
As in Heaven would float some PLEIAD,
In the hyaline embayèd,
   Anchored near him on the shore.

Then he cried out broken-hearted—
Ever true to the departed—
In this desert-world deserted—
 " Are we not to meet, dear Maiden !
  In the Rosy Bowers of AIDEN,
 As we did in Days of Yore ?"
And the voice of that sweet Maiden,
From the Jasper Reeds of Aiden,
With her lily-lips love-laden,
 Answered, " Yes ! forever more !"
And the old-time Towers of Aiden
 Echoed, " Yes ! forever more !"

VIII.

Like pure living Pearl she floated,
Looking now like one devoted
Unto death, which she denoted
 By the aspect that she wore ;
When his soul with her delighted,
For the loss of one benighted—
Wishing now to be requited—
 Ventured near her on the shore—
Where the willow wept above her
On the stream which seemed to love her,
For the soul that now did move her
 Was the love of his LENORE—
As this silver shining VESPER,
In among the Reeds of JASPER,
Wailed aloud for her sweet HESPER
 Who to Heaven had gone before !
For this heavenly-sweet Madonna,
In the Bowers of Chalcedony,
Used the plaintive voice of Cona
 Her Elysian chant to pour.

Then he cried out broken-hearted—
In this desert-world deserted—
Ever true to the departed—
    " Are we not to meet, dear Maiden !
    In the Rosy Bowers of AIDEN
    As we did in Days of Yore ?"
And the voice of that sweet Maiden,
From the emerald groves of Aiden,
With her lily-lips love-laden,
    Answered, " Yes ! forever more !"
And the old-time Towers of Aiden
    Echoed, " Yes, forever more !"

IX.

Then he asked her in his sorrow,
" Will you come to me to-morrow,
That my soul may solace borrow
    For the loss of my LENORE ?
I will tell you all the story
Of the Maiden now in glory—
For my soul is very sorry !
    Will you stay beside this shore ?"
When, her pearly bosom panting,
His request in silence granting,
As if what he wished was wanting—
    Her Elysian chant did pour
In such deep melodious thunder
That his grief was torn asunder—
All his soul was filled with wonder,
    Such as Man ne'er felt before—
Pouring out her soul, in sighing,
To persuade him from relying
On the DEMON who was trying
    To seduce him from LENORE.
    1*

Then he cried out joyful-hearted—
Feeling now no more deserted—
Ever true to the departed—
  " Are we not to meet, dear Maiden !
    In the Rosy Bowers of AIDEN,
  As we did in Days of YORE ?"
And the voice of that sweet Maiden,
From the Jasper Groves of AIDEN,
With her lily-lips love-laden,
  Answered, " Yes ! forever more !"
And the old-time Towers of Aiden
  Echoed, " Yes ! forever more !"

                  X.

Then, like living snow uplifted,
Like an Angel heavenly-gifted,
She again through Heaven was drifted
  On the saintly wings she wore,
Her sweet Seraph-song down-pouring
On his thirsting soul, upsoaring
In such Angel-like adoring,
  That the world seemed flooded o'er—
Rivers of deep song outwelling
From her saintly soul, foretelling
To POLITIAN—her own knelling—
  The return of Days of Yore—
Lofty piles of echoing thunder,
Filling all the sky Heaven under—
Drowning all the stars with wonder—
  Burthened with the name LENORE !
Till her joyful jubilation
Died in echoes through creation—
Leaving him in desolation—
  Darker—deeper than before !

Then he cried out broken-hearted,
In this desert-world deserted—
Ever true to the departed—
    " Are we not to meet, dear Maiden !
      In the Rosy Bowers of AIDEN,
    As we did in Days of Yore ?"
And the lips of that damned DEMON,
Like the Syren to the Seamen,*
With the voice of his dear LEMAN,
    Answered, " Never—never more !"
And the old-time Towers of Aiden
    Echoed, " Never—never more !"

XI.

Then, beside the silent river,
Where he wandered still forever,
By her lonely grave that ever
    Seemed to Heaven the only door—
Praying God to be forgiven—
In the twilight of the even—
Suddenly there came from Heaven,
    Dressed in saintly white, LENORE !
Like some saintly lily blowing,
In its fiery perfume glowing,
Light-invested, now bestowing
    On the Night its radiant lore—
This sweet Angel-Moon so tender,

---

* Sir Thomas Brown says, " What song the Syrens sung, or what name Achilles assumed when he hid himself among the women, though puzzling questions, are not beyond all conjecture."

" The Syrens were Sea Nymphs, who charmed so much with their melodious voice, that all forgot their employments to listen with more attention, and, at last, died from want of food. They were three in number, called Parthenope, Ligeia, and Leucosia; and they usually lived on a small Island near Cape Polorus, in Sicily."

Happy now his soul to render,
Clothed in Heaven's divinest splendor,
  Came to shine on earth's dark shore.
Seeing now the long-departed,
Quickly from the grave he started,
Crying out now joyful-hearted—
  " *God of Heaven! is this* LENORE ?
Are we not to dwell, dear Maiden!
In the Rosy Bowers of AIDEN,
With our souls all overladen
  With the joys that were of Yore ?"
And that glorified sweet Maiden,
From the Heavenly Bowers of AIDEN,
With her lily-lips love-laden,
  Answered, " Yes! forever more !"
And the God-built Towers of AIDEN
  Echoed, " Yes! forever more !"

XII.

Then he fell on earth before her,
On his knees there to adore her—
Praying God now to restore her,
  As she was in Days of Yore—
When she said to him, " POLITIAN !
Thou hast seen the heavenly Vision !
In the Flowery Fields Elysian
  Angels wait for thy LENORE !
Many Winters, many Summers,
Joys like this have been kept from us—
I have now fulfilled my promise—
  Oft fulfilled on earth before !
I have prayed for thy dear spirit—
Thou shalt Heaven above inherit—
Those rewards which thou dost merit—
  For the good kept aye in store.

I have prayed for thee in Heaven—
All thy sins are now forgiven—
Thou art pardoned—thou art shriven—
    O! forget not thy LENORE!"
Then he cried out joyful-hearted—
Never more to feel deserted—
As if they had never parted—
    " Are we not to meet, dear Maiden!
        In the Heavenly Bowers of AIDEN,
        On the Asphodelian shore ?"
And that glorified sweet Maiden,
From the Heavenly Bowers of AIDEN,
With her lily-lips love-laden,
    Answered, " YES! FOREVER MORE!"
And the God-built Towers of AIDEN
    Echoed, " Yes! forever more!"

XIII.

" God has now the day appointed
When thy soul shall be anointed—
By the Angels they are counted—
    All thy days on this dark shore.
O! be happy, I entreat thee!
I will come again to meet thee—
Sister Angels, too, shall greet thee—
    Crying, *Rise with thy* LENORE!
Through the luminiferous Gihon,*

---

* Gihon is one of the four rivers which watered the GARDEN OF EDEN.
I have made use of it here as signifying the Ether. In an old book
which I bought some years ago, entitled " *The True Knowledge of God
and Man,*" I find the following remarkable sentence : " The first part,
or river, is Pison, which compasseth the whole land of Havillah. This
is the universal Spirit which causes every thing to grow. It is the ele-

To the Golden City high on
High Eternity's Mount Zion,
 God-built in the Days of Yore—
To the Golden Land of Goshen,
Far beyond Time's upper ocean,*
Where, beholding our devotion,
 Float the argent Orbs all o'er—
To Avillion's happy Valley,
Where the breezes ever dally
With the Roses in each Alley—
 There to rest forever more."
Then he cried out joyful-hearted—
Never more to feel deserted—
Happy now with the departed—
 " Then we are to meet, dear Maiden !
 In the Heavenly Bowers of Aiden
 On the Asphodelian shore ?"
And that glorified sweet Maiden,
From the Heavenly Bowers of Aiden,

---

ment of fire, which produces precious gold, not only that of this earth,
but particularly the red sulpher of the sun—of Man ; and Bdellium ; and
also the transparent stone Onyx, the outside of which shines like gold,
but its inside is (שָׁמַיִם) *Shaumayim.* The second part, or river, is
Gihon. *This is the air,* which derives, or is derived, from the fire, and is
the fourth day's work. It compasses (not only *the whole land* of the
Moors, but) this whole *Chus,* or dry Earth. The third is called Hidde-
kel, *and goeth* (not towards the Assyrian land, but) towards the East.
Now, this East *is* the Sun. This Hiddekel, as the word signifies, is this
very Earth itself. The fourth is the Euphrates. This means all waters
together, to refresh again this whole burnt up *Chus,* or Earth !"

 * " It was imagined by some of the Ancients that there is an ethereal
ocean above us, and that the sun and moon are two floating luminous
islands, in which the spirits of the blest reside. Accordingly we find
that the word Ωχεανος was sometimes synonymous with αηρ, and death
was not unfrequently called Ωχεανοιο πορος, or *the passage of the ocean.*"

With her lily-lips love-laden,
　Answered, " Yes ! forever more !"
And the God-built Towers of AIDEN
　Echoed, " Yes ! forever more !"

XIV.

Then she said to him, " POLITIAN !
Thou hast seen the Heavenly Vision !
In the Flowery Fields Elysian
　Angels wait for thy LENORE.
Soon thy burning, star-like spirit
Shall the joys of Heaven inherit—
Those rewards which thou dost merit,
　Such as none have reaped before—
Where the glory-circled Sages,
Living sunlights to the Ages,
Golden Songs on silver pages
　Sing aloud on Salem's shore.
But if thou wouldst live forever,
Be thine own IDEAL ever,
And depart from Nature never,
　Her sweet absence to deplore !"
When, with Angel-like adoring,
She to Heaven again went soaring—
All his soul from Hell restoring—
　There to rest forever more !
Then he cried out broken-hearted—
Left again on earth deserted—
Ever true to the departed—
　" Are we not to meet, dear Maiden !
　　In the Heavenly Bowers of AIDEN
　On the Asphodelian shore ?"
And the lips of that damned Demon,
Like the Syren to the Seamen,

With the voice of his dear LEMAN,
    Answered, " Never—never more !"
And the old-time Towers of AIDEN
    Echoed, " Never—never more !"

XV.

Then, beside the silent river
Where he wandered still forever,
By her lonely grave that ever
    Seemed to Heaven the only door—
Came foul Lucifer returning
Up from Hell again all burning,
Through the amethystine morning,
    This infernal chant to pour :
" I will lead thee, my POLITIAN,
To the Flowery Fields ELYSIAN,
Where now waits the Heavenly Vision,
    Such as none have seen before.
There her lovely form reposes
On her bed of new-blown roses,
While the Angels scatter posies
    All that lily-form right o'er."
Then he cried out broken-hearted—
Ever true to the departed—
Left again on earth deserted—
    " Are we not to meet, dear Maiden !
    In the Heavenly Bowers of AIDEN
On the Asphodelian shore ?"
And the lips of that damned DEMON,
Like the Syren to the Seamen,
With the voice of his dear Leman,
    Answered, " Never—never more !"
And the old-time Towers of Aiden
    Echoed, " Never—never more !"

XVI.

" I will lead thee, my POLITIAN,
To this blessed Heavenly Vision
In the Flowery Fields Elysian,
    Such as none have seen before—
To the Blessed Land of GOSHEN,
Through the world-surrounding ocean,
Where the stars, in spheric motion,
    Music make on Heaven's bright shore.
Come—now taste this heavenly Lethe—
All the stars will seem beneath thee—
Thy LENORE will then seem with thee,
    As she was in Days of Yore.
Opening all thy inward senses,
It will lift thee up in trances,
Where the ANGEL-EXCELLENCES
    Sing aloud on Salem's shore—
Through the hyaline deep Ether,
Grapes of glory there to gather
In the bosom of thy FATHER,
    Where now rests thy lost LENORE !"
Then he cried out broken-hearted—
Ever true to the departed—
In this desert-world deserted—
    " Are we not to meet, dear Maiden !
      In the Heavenly Bowers of AIDEN
    On the Asphodelian shore ?"
And the lips of that damned DEMON,
Like the Syren to the Seamen,
With the voice of his dear Leman,
    Answered, " Never—never more !"
And the old-time Towers of Aiden
    Echoed, " Never—never more !"

XVII.

Then thus answered calm POLITIAN :
" If thou art this great Physician,
Better then thine own condition,
    Lifting thee from Hell's dark shore !
If I find you reap the treasure
Recommended in your measure,
I will drink with you with pleasure—
    But, kind stranger ! *not* before !
When the TRUTH shall hurl in terror
Down to Hell the demon ERROR,
Souls of men will then see clearer—
    Clear as Adam did of yore ;
For, it is by living purely,
That man's soul shall know as surely
He shall Heaven possess securely
    After death forever more."
Then he looked the agonizing
That he felt within him rising,
For the TRUTH was on him seizing—
    Making Hell in his heart's core !
Then he cried out broken-hearted—
Ever false to the DEPARTED—
By his own soul now deserted—
    " Are we not to damn, dear Maiden !
      In the Rosy Bowers of AIDEN,
   His proud soul forever more ?"
And the voice of that vile Maiden,
From the Rosy Bowers of AIDEN,
With her lying lips lust-laden,
    Answered, " Yes—forever more !"
And the old-time Towers of Aiden,
    Echoed, " Yes—forever more !"

XVIII.

" Hopeless fiends of wrath infernal !
Rise from out thy gloom eternal !
Drag POLITIAN's soul supernal
    Down to Hell's abyssmal shore !
Hear ye not the thundrous surging
Of their iron wings emerging
From Hell's craggy mouth, while scourging
    Back the darkness as they soar ?
Like an earthquake crawling under
This dark world in steps of thunder—
Striking kingdoms dumb with wonder !
    Hear ye not the wild uproar ?"
" *Let them come !*" POLITIAN thundered,
(While the Devil mutely wondered,
As within himself he pondered,
    What great wrath he had in store—)
" If destruction be their pleasure,
They shall have it without measure,
In deep Hell to reap the treasure
    Thou didst reap in Days of Yore !"
Then he cried out broken-hearted—
Ever false to the departed—
By his own soul still deserted—
    " What are we to do, dear Maiden !
    In the Rosy Bowers of AIDEN,
    With POLITIAN ?—nothing more ?"
And the voice of that frail Maiden,
From the Rosy Bowers of AIDEN,
With her trembling lips grief-laden,
    Answered, " *Nothing—nothing more !*"
And the old-time Towers of Aiden
    Echoed, " *Nothing—nothing more !*"

XIX.

" Back to Hell again in terror !
There repent thee of thine error—
Trying thus to make me sharer
 Of thy guilt to reap thy sore !
Lest God's wrath around thee blazing,
(All thy soulless soul amazing,)
Leave thee—all thy dark throne razing—
 Lightning-tortured ever more !
Back to Hell again to languish
Out thy future years in anguish !
Say, POLITIAN's soul did vanquish
 Thee, untouched by thy damned lore !
Tell the Heaven-rejoicing story,
That POLITIAN's soul, before ye,
Never bowed to lose the glory
 Kept in Heaven by his LENORE !"
" Then have I most vainly striven !
Baffled by the POWER OF HEAVEN !
Down to Hell by VIRTUE driven !
 Down to torment doubly sore !"
Thus with bitter lamentation
Did the DEMON OF DAMNATION
Shrink to Hell in consternation,
 There to wail forever more !
While around the Towers of AIDEN,
With her own guilt over-laden,
Wailed aloud the sinful Maiden,
 Crying, " *Yes ! forever more !*"
And all Hell—the Towers of Aiden—
 Echoed, " *Yes ! forever more !*"

XX.

Like an Angel swiftly flying
Down from Heaven to Virtue dying
In her innocence, loud-crying,
    " *God ! have mercy ! me restore !*"
From the Golden Land of GOSHEN,
Chariot-borne, with gentle motion,
Like the young Moon to the Ocean—
    To POLITIAN came LENORE—
Holy Angels her attending—
Singing, shouting, in descending—
Singing of the joys unending,
    For POLITIAN kept in store—
Crying out to him, " POLITIAN !
See ! behold the HEAVENLY VISION
From the Flowery Fields ELYSIAN !
    Rise to Heaven with thy LENORE !
To that GOLDEN CITY high on,
High ETERNITY'S MOUNT ZION,
Type of that which CHRIST did die on,
    Earth's lost Eden to restore !"
Then he cried out joyful-hearted—
Never more to feel deserted—
Never more to be Death-parted—
    " I will go with thee, sweet Maiden !
      To the Heavenly Bowers of AIDEN
    On the Asphodelian shore !"
And that glorified sweet Maiden
From her Chariot over Aiden,
With her lily-lips love-laden,
    Said, " TO REST FOREVER MORE !"
And the Heavens, high over Aiden,
    Echoed—" REST FOREVER MORE !"

XXI.

Thus she came to him descending,
Holy Angels her attending,
Singing of the joys unending
    For POLITIAN kept in store
While the SERAPHIM all waited
At the Portals congregated
Of the City Golden-gated,
    Crying, " RISE WITH THY LENORE !"
When, from out his clayey prison
Rose the soul of pure POLITIAN,
There to join the HEAVENLY VISION
    Glory-circled on the shore !
And, with life immortal gifted,
In her Chariot earthward drifted,
On the wings he wore uplifted,
    Entered joyful with the four.
Then, from earth, so long benighted,
Glorified, redeemed, requited,
In her Chariot, Angel-lighted,
    Soared POLITIAN with LENORE—
Crying out, now joyful-hearted—
Never more to feel deserted—
Never more to be Death-parted—
    " WE ARE GOING NOW, SWEET MAIDEN !
      To THE HEAVENLY BOWERS OF AIDEN
    ON THE ASPHODELIAN SHORE !"
While that glorified sweet Maiden,
Soaring up to HEAVENLY AIDEN,
With her lily-lips love-laden,
    Sang rejoicing ever more—
Entering into HEAVENLY AIDEN,
    There to rest forever more.

THE MIGHTY DEAD.

AN ELEGIAC POEM.

"Requiem æternam dona eis, Domine, et lux perpetua luceat eis."—*Chant of the Franciscan Monks over the Dead*

—

"Mourn for the mourner and not for the dead; for he is at rest, and we in tears."
—*From an Ancient Hebrew Dirge.*

—

"Thy sun shall no more go down; neither shall the moon withdraw herself; for the Lord shall be thine everlasting light, and the days of thy mourning shall be ended."—*Bible.*

—

I.

EVER—forever more—
Still upward—onward into perfect bliss—
  Dove-like thy spirit soars* to find that shore—
The ELYSIAN-Isle of JOY—where happiness
  And life are one—where man shall ever be
  Glorious in bliss—God-like eternally.

II.

Into that Far-off Land—
The ELYSIAN-Isles of INFINITE DELIGHT—
  Singing sweet anthems with that Angel-band
Around God's throne, whose souls, like Stars at night,
  Make music while they shine—thy soul is gone—
  Leaving the friends who mourn for thee alone!

III.

In that Serene Abode—
The EDEN-Isles of LOVE—thou art at rest—
  Safe in the Living Paradise of GOD—
Holding communion with the Heavenly Blest—

* William Henry Harrison.

Chanting sweet Spirit-songs of rapturous praise
With Heaven's high Seraphs, praising God always.

IV.

Swift as the rolling spheres
Diffuse their circular orbit-tones on high—
   Spreading till they embrace th' Eternal Years
With their dilating, wave-like melody—
   Winnowing the calm, clear, interstellar air—
   Does thy sweet, spiritual music spread up there.

V.

There, Amaranthine Flowers,
Immortal, grow, which never cease to bloom ;
   But, from the Evergreen Celestial Bowers,
Feed the bright Angels with divine perfume ;
   While, garmented with plumage ever gay,
   Ten thousand birds sing through Eternal Day.

VI.

There, Bowers of Asphodel
Breathe in th' Elysian air divine perfume—
   Sweet, Sylvan Homes, where wedded spirits dwell
Soon after they unite beyond the tomb—
   Couched upon Swan-down, where the Sylvanry
   Is sweeter than the Bowers of Œnoe.

VII.

Far, through the crsytal air,
Æolian sounds are heard, forever sweet,—
   Caused by the harp-like boughs which vibrate there,
Beneath the azure Breezes, when they meet,
   Soft Angels of the Spring ! to bear perfume
   From opening flowers to Seraphs as they bloom.

VIII.

On every leaf that grows
Beside the Living Waters, in each flower,
  A Song is written, which, while opening, shows
An Angel's history, which, sung, gives power
  To those who hear to know the things to be,
  And see that which before they could not see.

IX.

The soft light of their eyes
Shepherd the soul into the Folds of Bliss,
  Where the Green Pastures lie of Paradise—
(As Beauty's eyes have done the soul of this—)
  Where, lamb-like, they recline beneath some tree,
  Listening to hear the Doves sing joyously.

X.

Their language, too, is soft—
Continuous—flowing—like some gentle brook
  At midnight singing—heard by me so oft
In mine own land, when in some owlet-nook
  I lingered, listening to its flow at night,
  Beneath the Moon whose beams rained down delight.

XI.

There, streams forever flow,
Of crystal purity, which wind among
  The lawny, labyrinthine aisles, where blow
Unfading flowers—where birds, of various song,
  Sing, through unending Day, the Song of Love,
  And all that sing sing sweeter than the Dove.

2

XII.

All that could die is dead !
Thy body is as senseless as the grave !
 But thy undying Soul to Heaven hast fled—
A spiritual body—Christ alone could save !
 A perfect being, without parts—one whole—
 Is now the nature of thy God-made soul.

XIII.

And that which is thus made
Can never change—an essence can not die—
 An undivided whole can never fade—
But must endure forever—live on high
 When all that is of parts must fade away,
 And pass to those as subject to decay.

XIV.

Sorrow there can be none
Where the exalted splendor of the soul
 Shall shine out brighter than the noonday-sun !
For Death has over Spirits no control,
 And cannot touch Man's mind, nor mar the joy
 Of that which God himself will not destroy.

XV.

Then, what is Death ?—Not even
A common darkness which might here molest
 The soul in passing from this world to Heaven ;
That Valley of the Mountains of the Blest,
 From whose top God's immortal Son sublime
 Brought Truths to Man which thunder through all time.

XVI.

The grave is, then, the Gate
Which leads up to the Portals of that King
Whose House is Heaven—whose Temple is so great—
So wide—so lofty—high—that every thing
Th' Immortal Soul requires is there—divine—
And part of every thing that is, is thine.

XVII.

Like Moses on the Mount
Of HOREB, wonderful to look upon—
All garmented, with glory from the Fount
Of GOD—thou didst appear, great WASHINGTON!
Grasping the Parchment Scroll of LIBERTY,
Signed by the fearless Elders of the Free.

XVIII.

Thou wert the Great High Priest
Of Him who was the Prophet of the Free—
Who entered, as the follower of CHRIST,
The NEW JERUSALEM of LIBERTY,
And swore an oath which shook the dome of **Heaven,**
Never to rest till England's chains were **riven.**

XIX.

As on Oblivion
God laid the Corner Stone of Nature, which
The Fabric of this world was reared upon,
With such immeasurable grandeur rich
And wonderful in glory—so did they
Their Altar, built for LIBERTY, that Day.

XX.

And in this Country vast—
This great America—the Pride of Heaven !
Built of the columns of the ruined Past—
This Altar stood, where Tyrants' chains were riven,
  And FREEDOM's laws established by the Free,
  While offering up their hearts to LIBERTY.

XXI.

Their Orisons to pay,
Gathered the Constellations of the Free—
The Thirteen Sovereign States, who helped to lay
Their great Palladium's Corner Stone, to be
  To Future Generations all that they,
  For LIBERTY, had sacrificed that Day.

XXII.

This Monumental Fane,
As did the uncreated world in God's—
Lived archetypal in the souls of men ;
Till, springing upward from the dim abodes
  Of THOUGHT, it stood, like NATURE on the Night
  Of Chaos, wonderful—star-spangled—bright !

XXIII.

And this is FREEDOM's Home—
Adown whose sculpture-columned aisles there rolls—
(Peopling, with living Thought, the years to come—)
Man's eloquence in thunders !—to all souls,
  Like an inspired Rhapsodist, sublime,
  Speaking Life's Cyclic Poem through all time.

XXIV.

David, whose harp was strung
In ZION for the service of the LORD,
   Went up to Heaven before he died, with tongue
Lisping God's holy name—shouting that Word
   Which loosed the Nations from Barbarity,
   And made them live the Allies of the Free.

XXV.

That Word shall sleep no more,
Until the Ocean-song of his great soul
   Shall waft the waves of Truth to every shore—
Greening Man's soul with virtue as they roll—
   Till all the nations of the world are taught
   The billowy thunder-songs of his pure thought.

XXVI.

And that same Principle—
Long imaged forth in words of Living Truth
   Upon MESSIAH's lips—in quivering accents fell
From our forefathers, who, in deathless youth,
   Planted on Plymouth's barren Rock the Tree
   Which bore the First Fruits of our Liberty.

XXVII.

This principle lived still
In Nature, like the lightning in the air,
   Unseen, yet strong—awaiting but the will
To thunder—when oppression was stript bare—
   To utter nakedness—debased with guilt—
   Blasted with infamy—for blood long spilt.

XXVIII.

Thy soul, intent to hear,
Caught up the echoes of that Wondrous Voice—
  From soul to soul, as light from star to star,
Rolling—till all were radiant to rejoice—
  And through the labyrinthine aisles of earth
  Spread the Great Truths which now are going forth.

XXIX.

The troubled multitude,
Like Ocean impulsed by the Whirlwind's breath,
  Or Hurricane, in the Autumnal wood,
Gathering the scattered leaves round Summer's death—
  (As if the buried ages waked from sleep—)
  Wondered that Truth so clear should be so deep!

XXX.

The lever once applied—
Whose fulcrum was the ROCK of AGES—moved
  The multitude to undulations!—wide
As is the world, that Wondrous Voice reproved
  The guilty!—dove-winged for the years to come,
  It now goes forth the Future to call home.

XXXI.

As Genius gathers fame
As Time rolls on—never to die on earth—
  Till this broad world is peopled with his name—
(Circling creation in its goings forth,
  Like radiance round the sun—) so will the TRUTH,
From Voice to Voice, live in eternal youth.

XXXII.

What SHILOH uttered then—
Now eighteen hundred years ago—whose tones
   Are still vibrating in the minds of men,
Like lightning, in the thunder-peopled zones—
   Shaking the earth it purifies—which rolls
   As cradled upon sound—thy soul of souls

XXXIII.

Re-echoed to the Land !
And, whirlwind-like, upon th' opprobrious earth,
   Blew down Sin's Upas-tree, which dared withstand
The hurricane of thought, in going forth—
   As lightning from its thunder-sheath made bare,
   Withers the Oak it leaves forever sere.

XXXIV.

Up to the rolling spheres
It went, mingling with star-tones, which the Days
   Repeated to the Months—the Months to Years—
(As Night to Night went forth to offer praise—)
   The Years to Ages—Ages to all Time—
   Time to Eternity—in tones sublime.

XXXV.

Ignorance, then, howling, fled
Before the Light of Knowledge, as the Night
   Before the steps of DAY—till, blindly led,
She sank in TRUTH's deep sea—far out right—
   Whose waves closed round her, as the waves around
   Th' Egyptian Cohorts in the Red Sea drowned !—

XXXVI.

That glorious Nightingale,
Who sang of Life, Death, Immortality,
  With such celestial sweetness that the Vale
Of Death ran liquid music—Where is he?
  He who was Young by name, as through all time—
  Kindling the Stars with eloquence sublime?

XXXVII.

Where is that tuneful Tongue—
Religion's Cicero—who set the soul on fire
  With words of immortality?—who wrung
Confession from the Atheist's lips?—that Lyre,
  Whose strings were deathless thoughts, which shed
  Immortal music on the soul?—Not dead—

XXXVIII.

Alive—alive in Heaven!
Leader of that Seraphic Host which sing
  God's praises through the Eden-bowers of Even—
Drinking refreshing draughts from that sweet Spring
  Which flows out of God's Everlasting Sea
  To green the Joy-fields of Eternity.

XXXIX.

The thunder of his song
Reverberates through all High Heaven afar,
  Sprinkling his genius, as it rolls along,
In sweet, melodious rain, as if some star
  Had scattered down its sphered song in light,
  Dissolving gloriously the gloom of night.

XL.

Like that Sorrowful Tree,*
Whose blossoms only flourish in the night,
   Making the silence fragrant with its sea
Of odor—clouding darkness with the light
   Of moon-lit incense—thou didst Heaven divine
   With Music's love-unfolded Eglantine.

XLI.

Milton, that blind old " Sire
Of an immortal strain," for FREEDOM sung,
   Woke up the sleeping Nations with his Lyre—
Uttering deep TRUTHS, which died not on his tongue,
   Till LIBERTY's fierce torch, like Dragon's tongues,
   Had set each soul on fire to know his wrongs.

XLII.

That blind REPUBLICAN
First showed the hireling† of Charles Stuart's Court
   That LIBERTY belonged to every Man—
That Prelacy was but the Devil's sport
   To damn more souls—that all fiducial power
   Was vested in the PEOPLE as their Dower.

---

* " In the Island of Goa, near Bombay, there is a singular vegetable called the SORROWFUL TREE, because it only flourishes in the night. At sunset no flowers are to be seen, and yet, half an hour after, it is quite full of them. They yield a sweet smell; but the sun no sooner begins to shine upon them, than some of them fall off, and others close up, and thus it continues flowering in the night during the whole year."—*Payne's Universal Geography.*

† Salmasius.

2*

XLIII.

His fame shall outlive years ;
For as some cloud is broken into rain
    By lightning, her vile heart was into tears
By his immortal, soul-uplifting strain,
      Radiant with holy love, which, from his soul,
      In living thunders, burst from pole to pole.

XLIV.

Byron, that Bird of JOVE,
Perched on the Andes of immortal fame,
    Called to the prostrate Nations from above,
To rise aloft in LIBERTY's great name,
      And dash the clanking chains down from their slaves,
      Trampling the bones of Tyrants in their graves !

XLV.

Greece heard his welcome voice,
And kept the famished Anarch-wolves at bay,
    Howling around her with obstreperous noise,
Ready to tear her heart out as their prey—
      And cursed the hour that ever she was given
      To fatten dogs—the meanest under Heaven.

XLVI.

As when some mighty Crane,
With outstretched wings, scourging some thunder-cloud,
    When chariotted by tempests from the main—
Upborne by whirlwinds, screaming now aloud,
      Disturbs the stillness of the noontide air—
      Was Europe by the voice of her despair !

XLVII.

Marco Botzaris—he
Who heard the thunder-shout afar—rose up,
    And, by the trumpet-voice of LIBERTY,
Swore never more to drink the bitter cup
    Which pledged a Tyrant's health—when down it fell—
    Shattered to fragments on the Rock of Hell!

XLVIII.

Swords of Damascus steel
Gave he his hearts of oak, that Suliote Band,
    When they went forth at midnight, thus to deal
Destruction on the Tyrants of their land!
    And so he died, the bravest of the brave,
    When Tyranny sank with him to the grave.

XLIX.

Oh! as the red-hot tide
Gushed from his broken heart, the frightened earth
    Shook as when God was murdered! when he cried,
ENGLAND! PROTECT US!—But she came not forth!
    No—spurned him from her unmaternal breast!
    When did th' Oppressor ever aid th' opprest?

L.

Never were mortal men
More resolute—for they loved FREEDOM well,
    And longed to look upon her face again—
When Moslem's Hell-anointed Cohorts fell
    In hideous clangor round the path they trod,
    Like Chaos melting at the glance of God!

LI.

Shelly, that Human Dove,
Who hymned the DAWN OF LIBERTY with such
   Celestial sweetness, Angels from above
Bent down to hear him—whose ethereal touch
   So rained the soul of song out of his Lyre,
   They took him up to Heaven to lead their choir—

LII.

When his loud harp was strung,
His Halcyon thoughts, as when an Eagle springs,
   Winnowing the labyrinthine space among
The stars—glinting, with his aspiring wings,
   Their beams—with lightning swiftness thundered forth-
   Raining immortal music down on earth.

LIII.

On earth he sang of Love
And LIBERTY DIVINE, which cannot die ;
   And now enjoys the real bliss above
Of his Ideal here exultingly—
   While from his Amphionic harp the beams
   Of melody descend through Heaven in streams.

LIV.

The lightning of his song
Dissolves the heart of Genius into tears,
   As thunder shakes the world—until the wrong,
Which fed his soul with eloquence, appears
   Our own, while over what he sung we sigh,
   Mourning that any one so good could die !

LV.

And now he is in Heaven,
The ISRAFEL* among the Sons of Song,
    Like Hesperus among the Stars of Even—
Great Shepherd, folding his Celestial Throng,
    With lips all honeyed with the dews of love,
    Into the Paradise of Bliss above.

LVI

As yon bright Star of Even,
Ascending, kindling in its rapid flight,
    Forever to endure, till in High Heaven
It shines the CAPTAIN of the Host of Night;
    So did thy glory-circled spirit climb
    The Mount of Fame which overlooks all time.

LVII.

And there thy glorious form,
In Apotheosis Divine, shall stand,
    The gaze of Nations, while the thunder-storm
Shall sprinkle thee with lightnings, as thy hand,
    Spread out above the future years to-come,
    Shall beckon Genius to thy soul's pure home.

LVIII.

Thou, too, hast mourned, Sweet Dove!†
But wearest the aspect of immortal youth!
    Thou art like PEACE, begotten of Pure Love,
Nursed by RELIGION in the Bowers of Truth,
    And on Ambrosia, which the months do bring,
    Fed by the Spirit of Perpetual Spring.

---

* " The Angel Israfel, who has the most melodious voice of all God's creatures."—*Sale.*

† Felicia Hemans.

LIX.

Thou wert not born to die !
The grave could feel no pride in burying thee !
　　Death would not dare to look thee in the eye—
Or, if he did, those smiles of purity,
　　Like streams of light descending from above,
　　Would melt his icy heart to tears of love !

LX.

Thy songs have been to me
The bright unfoldings of that glorious hope
　　Which blossomed in immortal bloom in thee ;
Whose bud was, as young Passion burst it ope,
　　Frosted by Sorrow, which exhales perfume,
　　Of " tender smell," time never shall consume.

LXI.

A spirit-sounding sigh—
An aromatic sweetness of the heart,
　　Whose fragrant piety can never die—
Expressed in POETRY's Divinest art—
　　Was thy sweet Angel-music, full of love
　　And grief—deeper than Earth from Heaven above.

LXII.

Thy love was one deep sigh
Breathed from the depths of thine immortal soul—
　　Troubled with sorrow, which can never die,
While time shall last, or Music's waters roll
　　To grieve Man's heart with sorrow-joy—for how
　　Can Time affect that which delights him so ?

LXIII.

Like that sweet Bird of Night,*
Startling the ebon silence from repose,
   Until the stars appear to burn more bright
From its excessive gush of song, which flows
   Like some impetuous river to the sea—
   So thou did'st flood the world with melody.

LXIV.

For, as the Evening Star
Pants with its " silver lightnings" for the high
   And Holy Heavens—the Azure Calm afar—
Climbing with labor now the bending sky,
   To lead Night's Navy through the upper sea—
   So thou didst thirst for immortality.

LXV.

As underneath the sky,
Sad Autumn, the Religion of the year,
   Mourns that her sister Spring should ever die,
Whose summer-ripeness in the Fall grows sere,
   As beauty by the grave—so do we mourn
   For thee, Lost One ! who never canst return !—

LXVI.

Shakspeare, the God of Song,
Stands on the Pyramid of Sciences,
   Sublimely throned—with hand above the throng,
Who come to worship him, outstretched, to bless
   Their pilgrimage with wisdom from his store,
   Whose Archives are the world's collected lore.

---

* The Southern Mocking Bird.

LXVII.

The ocean deep of TRUTH
He sounded, sounded never so before—
  Bringing up PEARLS which an immortal youth
Had purchased him, which he, upon Time's shore,
  With liberal hand, has scattered, of great price
  To Man—worth more than Rubies to the Wise.

LXVIII.

From the deep Healing Wells
Of Wisdom, fathomed not by any line,
  Save his deep-diving thought, he plucked up Shells
Of such great price that they were called DIVINE,
  And such Celestial Music made, his name,
  Among th' ETERNAL, bought immortal fame.

LIX.

Wherever THOUGHT had been,
Searching on wildest wing for hidden Lore,
  He went, discursive, Eagle-winged, again,
And better found, where others searched before,
  Jewels, which they had left behind, which he
  Bestowed on Man for Immortality.

LXX.

That which the World thought best,
Was by his poorest bettered, till mankind
  Not only wondered how he was possessed
Of such great knowledge—feasting every mind,
  Already fat, to fatness—but how men
  Ever had lived without him until then.

LXXI.

His soul was like the sea,
Self-purifying, where his THOUGHTS, launched forth,
  Became the Jewel-laden Argossy—
Freighted with all the Merchandise of earth—
  Which he unloaded on the Wharf of Time—
  Piling it up in Mountain-heaps sublime.

LXXII.

Two hundred years ago,
Had he not lived, the World had been behind
  Two hundred years—the Present knows this so—
For all was Chaos, till his God-like Mind
  Moved on the formless nothing of the Past,
  When Wisdom's World stood forth, soul-girdled—vast!—

LXXIII.

We heard an Angel's wings
Hovering at night above thy* dying bed—
  Shaking sweet dews of comfort, as from strings
Of gold falls song, upon thy pillowed head—
  Making sweet music—soft as is the light
  Rained from the Moon upon the dark of night.

LXXIV.

And when thy breath was gone,
We heard him soaring to the Western Star !
  We listened to his music, *all* as one,
Till it was lost in silence in the air !
  When all grew still !—*so* still, that every breath
  Seemed stopt by that one glorious death !

* Andrew Jackson

LXXV.

We heard our own hearts beat,
And each the other's answered, as we stood
    Listening for those dumb accents, *once* so sweet ;
And feeling for those pulsings of rich blood
    Whose life-imparting properties were gone—
    Leaving thy heart within as cold as stone !

LXXVI.

Yes ! thou art now at rest !
The labor of thy Week of Life is done !
    And in the SABBATH of the skies, possessed
Of an immortal joy, thou art to run
    No more the race of glory, for the prize
    Of Heaven is won—how dazzling to thine eyes !

LXXVII.

Æons of Æons thou
Shalt live throned in thy Country's grateful heart—
    Forever more divine as thou art now—
A spirit never from her to depart ;
    For thou art with the TRUTH, which thou didst love,
    Coupled, as God is with the Heavens above.

LXXVIII.

For thou wert like, on earth,
That glorious Diamond* which the Shepherd found,
    Who looked upon it as of little worth ;
And as its Heavenly radiance scattered round
    His ignorant way the whitest beams of light,
    So thou didst Wisdom on the World's dark night.

---

* " This Diamond was found near Adrianople, among some ruins, by a Shepherd, who made use of it above a year to strike fire from to light his pipe. It was valued '' more than two hundred purses."—*A. De La Motray's Travels.*

LXXIX.

Dark—moaning in the wind—
The Cypress flings its shadow on his grave,
   Where lies the Temple of his mighty mind,
Whose glory is as bright as he was brave—
   The echo of whose name is heard afar—
   Far as the Eastern from the Western Star.

LXXX.

Never to come on earth—
Never to visit us in Time again—
   A spiritual body—thou shalt wanton forth
In endless being, righteous to remain—
   A God-anointed soul to live all pure,
   As long as His own life-time shall endure.

LXXXI.

Never to come again—
Never, while earth remains what it is now—
   Nor while the sunbeams fall from Heaven like rain,
To raise up flowers to deck her dusky brow ;
   Nor while the Stars shall their wide Cycles roll—
   Wilt thou return, great Chastener of the soul !

LXXXII.

We need not look for thee !
Thou hast fulfilled the object of thy birth,
   And been on earth what thou wert made to be—
A holy man—one, who adorned the earth,
   And made it better than it would have been,
   Hadst thou not lived—thou wilt not come again !

LXXXIII.

No, never will thy voice
Wake up the heart to ecstacies again !
   Nor make those who once loved thee here, rejoice
That thou wert born—whose absence now is pain !
   Not through the long, long trying years to-come,
   Wilt thou return to this, thy native home !

LXXXIV.

Farewell !—No more on earth,
Through all succeeding time, wilt thou be seen
   Among mankind ! for thou hast had one birth—
One death—the mother of that birth to men
   Which shall not die—for life to Man was given
   That he might pass through death to life in Heaven.

LXXXV.

Upon the Willow-tree,
Weeping above thy grave, my harp shall hang—
   Silent as death—till taken down by me
To sing again the DEAD, like him who sang
   For ADONAIS,* whom the World did wrong,
   With the swift thunders of his ORPHIC SONG.

---

* Shelley, the golden-mouthed Swan of Albion, who mourned for his
beloved friend Keats, in an Elegy entitled " ADONAIS."

The following beautiful lines, from the glorious Petrarch, are truly applicable to him :

> " In nobil sangue, vita umile e queta,
>   Ed in alto intelletto un puro core ;
>   Frutto senile in sul giovenil fiore,
>   E in aspetto pensoso, anima lieta."

AVALON.

" I will open my dark saying upon the Harp."—DAVID.

—

" All thy waves and billows are gone over me. I sink in deep mire where there is
no standing !"—PSALMS.

—

" There be tears of perfect moan
Wept for thee in Helicon."—MILTON.

—

I.

Death's pale cold orb has turned to an eclipse
 My Son of Love !
The worms are feeding on thy lily-lips,
 My milk-white Dove !
Pale purple tinges thy soft finger-tips !
While nectar thy pure soul in glory sips,
As Death's cold frost mine own forever nips !
  Where thou art lying
  Beside the beautiful undying
 In the valley of the pausing of the Moon,
Oh ! AVALON ! my son ! my son !

II.

Wake up, oh ! AVALON ! my son ! my son !
 And come from Death !
Heave off the clod that lies so heavy on
 Thy breast beneath
In that cold grave, my more than Precious One !
And come to me ! for I am here alone—
With none to comfort me !—my hopes are gone

Where thou art lying
Beside the beautiful undying
In the Valley of the pausing of the Moon,
Oh! AVALON! my son! my son!

III.

Forever more must I, on this damp sod,
    Renew and keep
My Covenant of Sorrows with my God,
    And weep, weep, weep!
Writhing in pain beneath Death's iron rod!
Till I shall go to that DIVINE ABODE—
Treading the path that thy dear feet have trod—
    Where thou art lying
    Beside the beautiful undying
In the Valley of the pausing of the Moon,
Oh! AVALON! my son! my son!

IV.

Oh! precious Saviour! gracious heavenly Lord!
    Refresh my soul!
Here, with the healings of thy heavenly Word,
    Make my heart whole!
My little Lambs are scattered now abroad
In Death's dark Valley, where they bleat unheard!
Dear Shepherd! give their Shepherd his reward
    Where they are lying
    Beside the beautiful undying
In the Valley of the pausing of the Moon,
With AVALON! my son! my son!

V.

For thou didst tread with fire-ensandaled feet,
    Star-crowned, forgiven,
The burning diapason of the stars so sweet,
    To God in Heaven!

And, walking on the sapphire-paven street,
Didst take upon the highest Sill thy seat—
Waiting in glory there my soul to meet,
 When I am lying
 Beside the beautiful undying
In the Valley of the pausing of the Moon,
Oh ! Avalon ! my son ! my son !

VI.

Thou wert my Micro-Uranos below—
 My Little Heaven !
My Micro-Cosmos in this world of wo,
 From morn till even !
A living Lyre of God who charmed me so
With thy sweet songs, that I did seem to go
Out of this world where thou art shining now,
 But without lying
 Beside the beautiful undying
In the Valley of the pausing of the Moon,
Oh ! Avalon ! my son ! my son !

VII.

Thou wert my son of Melody alway,
 Oh ! Child Divine !
Whose golden radiance filled the world with Day !
 For thou didst shine
A lustrous Diadem of Song for aye,
Whose Divertisments, through Heaven's Holyday,
Now ravish Angel's ears—as well they may—
 While I am crying
 Beside the beautiful undying
In the Valley of the pausing of the Moon,
Oh ! Avalon ! my son ! my son !

VIII.

Thy soul did soar up to the Gates of God,
   Oh ! Lark-like Child!
And through Heaven's Bowers of Bliss, by Angels trod,
   Poured Wood-notes wild !
In emulation of that Bird, which stood,
In solemn silence, listening to thy flood
Of golden Melody deluge the wood
     Where thou art lying
     Beside the beautiful undying
   In the Valley of the pausing of the Moon,
   Oh! AVALON ! my son ! my son !

IX.

Throughout the Spring-time of Eternity,
   Oh ! AVALON !
Pæans of thy selectest melody
   Pour forth, dear Son !
Clapping thy snow-white hands incessantly,
Amid Heaven's Bowers of Bliss in ecstasy—
The odor of thy song inviting me
     Where thou art lying
     Beside the beautiful undying
   In the Valley of the pausing of the Moon,
   Oh ! AVALON ! my son ! my son !

X.

The redolent quintessence of thy tongue,
   Oh ! AVALON !
Embowered by Angels Heaven's sweet Bowers among—
   Many in one—
Is gathered from the choicest of the throng,
In an Æonian Hymn forever young,
Thou Philomelian Eclecticist of Song !

While I am sighing
Beside the beautiful undying
In the Valley of the pausing of the Moon,
For AVALON! my son! my son!

XI.

Here lies dear Florence with her golden hair,
And violet eyes;
Whom God, because she was for earth too fair,
Took to the skies!
With whom my Zilly only could compare—
Or Eugene Percy, who was debonair,
And rivaled each in every thing most rare!
These now are lying
Beside the beautiful undying
In the Valley of the pausing of the Moon,
With AVALON! my son! my son!

XII.

Her eyes were like two Violets bathed in dew
From morn till even—
The modest Myrtle's blossom-Angel blue,
And full of Heaven.
Up to the golden gates of God she flew,
To grow in glory as on earth she grew,
Heaven's own primeval joys again to view—
While I am crying
Beside the beautiful undying
In the Valley of the pausing of the Moon,
Oh! AVALON! my son! my son!

XIII.

The Violet of her soul-suffused eyes
Was like that flower
Which blows its purple trumpet at the skies
For Dawn's first hour—

3

The Morning-glory at the first sunrise,
Nipt by Death's frost with all her glorious dyes!
For Florence rests where my dear Lily lies—
 Where thou art lying
 Beside the beautiful undying
 In the Valley of the pausing of the Moon,
Oh! AVALON! my son! my son!

XIV.

Four little Angels killed by one cold Death
 To make God glad!
Four Cherubs gone to God, the best he hath—
 And all I had!
Taken together, as if in His wrath,
While walking, singing, on Hope's flowery path—
Breathing out gladness at each odorous breath—
 Now they are lying
 Beside the beautiful undying
 In the Valley of the pausing of the Moon,
Oh! AVALON! my son! my son!

XV.

Thou wert like Taleisin,* "full of eyes,"
 Bardling of Love!
My beautiful Divine Eumenides!
 My gentle Dove!
Thou silver Swan of Golden Elegies!
Whose Mendelsohnian Songs now fill the skies!
While I am weeping where my Lily lies!
 Where thou art lying
 Beside the beautiful undying
 In the Valley of the pausing of the Moon,
Oh! AVALON! my son! my son!

---

* Taleisin, the Druidical High Priest, or Bard. Ezekiel, in describing
the great knowledge of the Cherubim, says, that they were "*full of eyes.*"

XVI.

Kindling the high-uplifted stars at even
  With thy sweet song,
The Angels, on the Sapphire Sills of Heaven,
  In rapturous throng,
Melted to milder meekness, with the Seven
Bright Lamps of God to glory given,
Leant down to hear thy voice roll up the leven,
    Where thou art lying
    Beside the beautiful undying
  In the valley of the pausing of the Moon,
  Oh! AVALON! my son! my son!

XVII.

Can any thing that Christ has ever said,
  Make my heart whole?
Can less than bringing back the early dead,
  Restore my soul?
No! this alone can make my Heavenly bread—
Christ's Bread of Life brought down from Heaven, instead
Of this sad Song, on which my soul has fed,
    Where thou art lying
    Beside the beautiful undying
  In the Valley of the pausing of the Moon,
  Oh! AVALON! my son! my son!

XVIII.

Have I not need to weep from Morn till Even,
  Far bitterer tears
Than cruel Earth, the unforgiven,
  Through his long years—
Inquisitorial Hell, or strictest Heaven,
Wrung from Christ's bleeding heart when riven?
Thus from one grief unto another driven,

Where thou art lying
Beside the beautiful undying
In the Valley of the pausing of the Moon,
Oh! AVALON! my son! my son!

XIX.

Yes! I have need to weep, to groan, to cry,
　　And never faint,
Till, battering down God's Golden Gates on high,
　　With my complaint,
I soften His great heart to make reply,
By sending my dear son from Heaven on high—
Or causing me in this dark grave to lie,
　　Where thou art lying
　　Beside the beautiful undying
In the Valley of the pausing of the Moon,
Oh! AVALON! my son! my son!

XX.

I see the BRIDEGROOM of the Heavenly Bride,
　　In robes of light!
My little ONES now stand his form beside,
　　In linen white!
Embowered by Angels, star-crowned, in their pride,
Singing Æonian songs in joyful tide—
Although much larger grown than when they died—
　　While I am sighing
　　Beside the beautiful undying
In the Valley of the pausing of the Moon,
Oh! AVALON! my son! my son!

THE LUSIAD.

" Si je te perds, je suis perdue."—*From a Cameo.*

I.

On the banks of Talapoosa,
　　Long time ago,
Where it mingles with the Coosa,
　　Southward to flow—
Dwelt the Maid I love, sweet Lucy!
　　Lucy, long time ago—
Bringing Heaven to earth, sweet Lucy!
　　Lucy, long time ago.
　　Ah! who now can know
How I loved the Maid, sweet Lucy!
　　Lucy, long time ago.

II.

Like the black wings of the Raven
　　In the sun's glow,
On her neck, from morn till even,
　　Whiter than snow,
Like fresh lilies born in Heaven—
　　Flowed her locks low—
(For they never had been shaven—)
　　Long time ago.
　　Ah! who now can know
How I loved the Maid, sweet Lucy!
　　Lucy, long time ago.

III.

Like the blue-eyed Morning-Glory
  When it doth blow
At the skies to tell the story
  Of the sun's glow
In the East when it is hoary—
  (Gladdening to know—)
Were her blue eyes—ever sorry
  Is my soul now!
  For, ah! who can know
How I loved the Maid, sweet Lucy!
  Lucy, long time ago.

IV.

Pure as when the Virgin Mary
  First came to know
That her heart was born to carry
  Christ here below—
Who was neither sad nor merry—
  Lucy looked now—
(Like the North Star not to vary—)
  Long time ago.
  Ah! who now can know
How I loved the Maid, sweet Lucy!
  Lucy, long time ago.

V.

Like the plaintive voice, in Summer,
  Of the Dove, low,
When her melting heart doth murmur
  Accents of wo
For the mate that is torn from her—
  (Golden in flow—)

Were the words of my sweet Lucy,
  Lucy, long time ago.
  Ah! who now can know
How I loved the Maid, sweet Lucy!
  Lucy, long time ago.

VI.

Like the young Fawn in the Valley,
  Seeking the Doe,
On the banks of Oostanalla,
  Gone with her Roe—
Came she down the Emerald Alley,
  Warbling words low,
Singing when she talked, sweet Lucy!
  Lucy, long time ago.
  Ah! who now can know
How I loved the Maid, sweet Lucy!
  Lucy, long time ago.

VII.

Like two roses ever blowing,
  Hued as they blow,
Were her bright cheeks ever glowing
  In her soul's glow—
As if Heaven were now bestowing
  All she did know
Of herself on my sweet Lucy,
  Lucy, long time ago.
  Ah! who now can know
How I loved the Maid, sweet Lucy!
  Lucy, long time ago.

VIII.

In the sweet time that was floral,
   With her lips so—
She this EONCH of sweet Coral
   Loudly did blow.
Now Heaven's never-fading laurel
   Crowneth her brow,
Where she went to dwell, sweet Lucy!
   Lucy, long time ago.
   Ah! soon you will know
Why I loved the Maid, sweet Lucy!
   Lucy, long time ago.

IX.

In the May-Moon, when I sought her
   Freely to know,
From the acromatic water,
   Ruby-tinct, low,
Did this Dian, Heaven's sweet Daughter,
   Bring to me now
This sweet EONCH, which I taught her
   Loudly to blow.
   Ah! *now* you can know
Why I loved the Maid, sweet Lucy!
   Lucy, long time ago.

X.

I was then her Triton truly,
   Truly as now—
This sweet EONCH, then so newly
   Found here below
In the stream that flowed on coolly,
   Freely to blow,

And reveal to Heaven as duly
   All I did know
Of the charms of my sweet Lucy,
   Lucy, long time ago.
   In words white as snow
Flowed the soul of my sweet Lucy,
   Lucy, long time ago.

XI.

In the mild month of October,
   As we did go
Through the Fields of Cooly Rauber,
   No one can know,
But the great Archangel Auber,
   What songs did flow—
(Bringing Heaven to earth to robe her
   In light like snow—)
From the lips of my sweet Lucy,
   Lucy, long time ago.
   Ah ! *now* you can know
Why I loved the Maid, sweet Lucy!
   Lucy, long time ago.

XII.

Like the young bud of the Tulip,
   Half hid in snow,
Just disparting of its blue lip—
   Looked her eyes now,
When I kissed the nectared julep
   From her lips *so*—
Blushing with my bashful Lucy,
   Lucy, long time ago.
   Ah ! who *now* can know
How I loved the Maid, sweet Lucy!
   Lucy, long time ago.
   3*

XIII.

Then from out the East low looming,
    Earthward, but slow,
A dark thunder-cloud came booming,
    Loud as the flow
Of ten thousand oceans spooming,
    Breaking below
Over mighty rocks, entombing
    People in wo!
    Ah! who now can know
How I feared for my sweet Lucy,
    Lucy, long time ago.

XIV.

Then the lightning fell in flashes,
    Laying her low!
Burning up her robes to ashes—
    Leaving me so!
While her soul stood there as fresh as
    The new-fallen snow—
A white Dove from out the meshes
    Of the world's wo—
Ready made for Heaven, sweet Lucy!
    Lucy, long time ago.
    Ah! *who* now can know
How I prayed for my sweet Lucy,
    Lucy, long time ago.

XV.

Round her form of beauty glowing,
    Glorified so,
Angel-robes of light were flowing,
    Whiter than snow,

All her radiant beauty showing
    Unto me now—
Heaven's own joys on her bestowing—
    On me—deep wo!
Ah ! now you can know
Why I mourned for my sweet **Lucy**,
    Lucy, long time ago.

XVI.

Then from out the depths of Heaven,
    Glorious in glow,
By an Angel's hand down-driven—
    (Horses of snow—)
A bright Chariot left the levin,
    Coming below—
Bearing back to God sweet **Lucy**,
    Lucy, long time ago.
Ah ! *now* you can know
Why I mourned for my sweet **Lucy**,
    Lucy, long time ago.

XVII.

On the banks of Talapoosa,
    Free from all wo,
Where it mingles with the Coosa,
    Southward to flow—
Rests my beautiful sweet **Lucy**
    In her grave low !
Taking Heaven from earth, sweet **Lucy** !
    Lucy, long time ago.
Ah ! now you can know
Why I mourned for my sweet **Lucy**,
    Lucy, long time ago.

XVIII.

Weeping willows bend above her,
  Where she lies low!
As if each one were her lover
  Burthened with wo!
Guardian Angels sent to hover
  Over her now,
As if striving to discover
  What none can know
But the one that loved sweet Lucy,
  Lucy, long time ago.
  Ah! *now* you can know
How I loved the Maid, sweet Lucy!
  Lucy, long time ago.

ISABEL;

BALLAD OF LOVE

I.

Saintly lilies mixed with roses
    Were thy cheeks, dear ISABEL!
Where my memory now reposes—
    Fare-thee-well!
Like the Dawn when it is snowing,
    Was thy lily-breast to me,
On my soul its sweets bestowing,
    Full of love—farewell to thee!

II.

Sorrow never—always pleasure
    Thou didst give me, ISABEL!
Poured upon me without measure—
    Fare-thee-well!
For thy soul it was the spirit
    Of the bliss that dwelt in me,
Such as those in Heaven inherit
    After death—farewell to thee!

III.

Sweeter than Hope's lute replying
    Unto Doubt, dear ISABEL!
Was thy voice to me when sighing—
    " FARE-THEE-WELL !"
Sweeter far than Swan left wailing—
    Dying on some Summer Sea—
Was thy song to me, foretelling
    This deep grief—farewell to thee!

IV.

When my head lay on the pillow
    Of thy breast, dear ISABEL!
Heaving like some milky billow—
    Fare-thee-well !
Then thy heart gushed overflowing
    From thine eyes too blind to see—
Washing out the roses blowing
    On thy cheeks—farewell to thee !

V.

Then thy heart to mine was beating,
    Full of pain, dear ISABEL !
Each fond pulse of mine repeating—
    Fare-thee-well !
Like the Moon through cloudy weather,
    Beamed thy countenance on me,
Through thy tears, as we together
    Wailed aloud—farewell to thee !

VI.

Then thine arms securely placing
    Round my neck, dear ISABEL!
Looked we not, when thus embracing—
    FARE-THEE-WELL ?

Thou didst look the agonizing
  Felt, I thought, by none but me,
When thy heart in tears gushed rising
  To thine eyes—farewell to thee!

VII.

Then in one long trance of feeling,
  Deep as Heaven, dear ISABEL!
All our love—our grief—revealing—
  Fare-thee-well!
There we clung—had clung forever,
  Had not Hope thus whispered me—
Thus to part is not to sever—
  Both are one—farewell to thee!

VIII.

Lonely, like the first-sent Raven
  From the Ark, dear ISABEL!
Wandered we from our soul's Haven—
  Fare-thee-well!
Then like our first parents driven
  Out of Eden, so were we—
Having now no home but Heaven—
  So we went—farewell to thee!

IX.

Though our bodies here are parted—
  Mine from thine, dear ISABEL!
Our two hearts are single-hearted—
  Fare-thee-well!
Farther we are separated,
  Nearer shall our spirits be—
Leaving space annihilated
  By our love—farewell to thee!

X.

Though we have been doomed to sever
    Here on earth, dear ISABEL !
Yet, it shall not be forever—
    Fare-thee-well !
Let us, then, some solace borrow
    From the thought that we shall be
Re-united, free from sorrow,
    After death—farewell to thee !

XI.

Though our hopes have all been blighted
    Here on earth, dear ISABEL !
We shall be in Heaven united—
    Fare-thee-well !
Budding joys, that blossom never
    Here on earth, in Heaven shall be
Made to flourish there forever,
    When we meet—farewell to thee !

XII.

Sweeter far than our first meeting
    Here on earth, dear ISABEL !
Shall be our eternal greeting—
    Fare-thee-well !
Parted is not disunited—
    Severed we can never be—
Thus in grief we are requited
    By our love—farewell to thee

XIII.

Flowery Islands stud the river
    Where we met, dear ISABEL !
There our aspen lips did quiver···
    " FARE-THEE-WELL !"

Nightly through the months of Summer,
   Keeping tryste, dear love! for me,
Thou didst wait to hear me murmur
   My true love—farewell to thee!

XIV.

But you dared not show your sorrow
   To your friends, dear ISABEL!
Nor from Hope one solace borrow—
   Fare-thee-well!
When they told thee I had perished,
   But to win thy soul from me,
All thy precious hopes, long cherished,
   Died away—farewell to thee!

XV.

All the solace you could borrow
   For your grief, dear ISABEL!
Was to wail aloud in sorrow—
   " FARE-THEE-WELL!"
From the rosy river-Islands
   Thou didst swim at night to see
If, by moonlight, on the Highlands,
   I had died—farewell to thee!

XVI.

On the name of thy true lover
   Thou didst call, dear ISABEL!
But thou couldst not him discover—
   Fare-thee-well!
There thy violet-eyes, all clouded
   With their tears, did seem to see
On the ground thy lover shrouded—
   Lying dead—farewell to thee!

XVII.

Wailing thus his name, distracted,
 Every night, dear ISABEL !
Friends were to the spot attracted—
 Fare-thee-well !
There they found thy body lying
 On the ground, when, suddenly,
Up they saw thy spirit flying
 Into Heaven—farewell to thee !

XVIII.

There thy body still kept lying
 On the ground, dear ISABEL !
While thy soul soared upward crying—
 " FARE-THEE-WELL !"
For thy voice grew shriller, shriller,
 Soaring up to Heaven for me ;
Then, at length, grew stiller—stiller—
 Silent now—farewell to thee !

XIX.

Every night they hear the wailing
 Of thy voice, dear ISABEL !
All their future grief foretelling—
 Fare-thee-well !
Still pursued—forever flying—
 Nothing of thy form they see;
But they hear the bitter crying
 Of thy soul—farewell to thee!

XX.

Nightly, through the months of Summer,
 Thou dost come, dear ISABEL !
To their tortured souls to murmur—
 " FARE-THEE-WELL !"

Haunted by thy Heavenly Spirit—
    Tortured here on earth—they see
Hell through life—Hell shall inherit
    After death—farewell to thee !

XXI.

When thy mother wanders crying—
    " *Where is my dear* ISABEL ?"
Echo comes to her replying—
    " FARE-THEE-WELL !"
All her joy is turned to sorrow,
    Thinking how she tortured me—
Solace none from Hope to borrow—
    All is Hell—farewell to thee !

XXII.

Underneath the Weeping Willow
    Thou dost sleep, dear ISABEL !
Lying on thy satin pillow—
    Fare-thee-well !
When thy saintly soul was ferried
    Over Death's dark, dismal sea,
Thy dear lily-form was buried
    In this grave—farewell to thee!

XXIII.

Flowers are blooming without number
    On thy grave, dear ISABEL !
Calling me to peaceful slumber—
    Fare-thee-well !
Angels from the shining Portal
    Of the Golden City, see
How we mourn the Young Immortal
    Gone to God—farewell to thee !

XXIV.

Last night, while my soul was talking
    To itself, dear ISABEL!
By my side came Memory walking—
    Fare-thee-well!
Back we wandered through the Wildwood,
    Where thy soul first came to me,
In the innocence of childhood,
    Full of love—farewell to thee!

XXV.

There we heard the joyful laughter
    Of the Youths, dear ISABEL!
Which my soul goes sighing after—
    Fare-thee-well!
Where the fairest of Earth's daughters
    Golden sands of Truth, with me,
Gathered from the shining waters
    Of our souls—farewell to thee!

XXVI.

Angel Days, in Heavenly Chorus,
    By us flew, dear ISABEL!
Singing of the joys before us—
    Fare-thee-well!
Joyful Birds, forever singing,
    Sported there from tree to tree,
While the woods were loudly ringing
    With their song—farewell to thee!

XXVII.

Like an Angel sweetly smiling
    On the earth, dear ISABEL!
All the night of care beguiling—
    Fare-thee-well!

Silver twilight softly snowing
  On the earth and on the sea,
All the darkness overflowing—
  Rode the Moon—farewell to thee !

XXVIII.

Velvet moss of emerald lustre
  Laced the Rocks, dear ISABEL !
Where the Golden Grapes did cluster—
  Fare-thee-well !
While the dazzling emerald-glowing
  Of the leaves upon each tree,
Verdant twilight there bestowing—
  Soothed the soul—farewell to thee !

XXIX.

Eden-flowers of richest odor,
  Just in bloom, dear ISABEL !
Made Mosaic all the border—
  Fare-thee-well !
Languid Lilies, newly blowing,
  Lolled upon the emerald lea,
All their virgin beauty showing
  To the Moon—farewell to thee !

XXX.

Thus we wandered through the Wildwood
  Where we roved, dear ISABEL !
In the innocence of childhood—
  Fare-thee-well !
All our talk had sunk to silence,
  Angel's language, when, to me,
Music came, as from the Highlands
  Up in Heaven—farewell to thee !

XXXI.

Listening, rapt with wonder, sighing,
  For the VOICE, dear ISABEL!
I beheld an angel flying—
  Fare-thee-well!
It was thy dear, Heavenly Spirit
  Coming down to say to me,
"THOU SHALT HEAVEN ABOVE INHERIT
  AFTER DEATH"—farewell to thee!

AGNUS;

OR,

THE LITTLE PET LAMB.

A PASTORAL.

"Feed my Lambs."—Christ's Charge to Peter.

I.

I never shall forget the day
I went to see sweet Alice Gray—
The little lamb that lived half way
To Heaven above—the child of May.
For near the path that led me by
The Plumtrees, on the ground did lie
A little lamb whose child-like cry
Told it had wandered there to die.

II.

Its mother wandering from the fold
When it was only three days old,
Was found upon the open wold,
Dead—dying of the bitter cold.
All day along the deep ravine,
Beside the rill that rolled between
Two sloping hills of emerald green,
Its little tiny tracks were seen.

III.

All night upon the emerald moss
That did the old gray rocks emboss,
Beside the stream it could not cross—
It lay lamenting its great loss!
In pale cold swoon, with dew bedight,
Low in the Moon's soft arms of light,
This lily lay in beauty bright
Snowing her whiteness on the night.

IV.

For as the little dappled Fawn,
Out of the lily-jeweled lawn,
At daybreak, eyes the milky Swan
Floating upon the Lake at dawn—
So did she from the emerald lea
Of this dark life gaze silently
At lambs beneath the Big Oak tree,
Sporting in joyful jubilee.

V.

Thus all day long adown the Vale
Vocal with her eternal wail,
She wandered sighing out her tale
Upon the suckle-scented gale.
Sometimes amid the verdant bowers,
Attended by the joyful Hours,
She scattered dew from off the flowers
Down on her limbs in pearly showers.

VI.

Thus orphaned on the dewy mead,
Self-exiled in her utmost need,
A weary, weary life indeed
Did she among the lilies lead

At noontide, with the wild Gazelles,
Amid the flowery Asphodels,
She learnt to drink from dewy wells
That fountained in the lily-bells.

VII.

The Fawn may seek the mountain Doe—
Down from the Hills may leap the Roe
To where the saintly lilies blow
All night upon the Vales below ;
The amorous Doe may come again
Back to the Isles of Jasper Cane ;
But for her mother, Death has slain,
She all night long shall wait in vain !

VIII.

For three long months in bitter cold,
With child-like plaint, it meekly told
Its sorrows to the snowy fold
That fleeced all night the open wold.
At midnight by the purling rill
That carolled down the echoing Hill,
She heard the plaintive Whippoorwill
Beg to be whipt—keeps begging still.

IX.

I took it from the place it lay,
And bore it to sweet Alice Gray—
The little Lamb that lived half way
To Heaven above—the Child of May.
It never, from the first, was wild,
But followed her like some sweet child,
With artless innocence so mild,
As meek as it was undefiled.

4

X.

Then in an ocean of green wheat
I placed it, that it there might eat,
Where, wading with its snowy feet,
Its happiness seemed now complete.
But how I loved that little lamb,
That played at evening in the calm
With Alice on sweet beds of balm—
Is only known to the I Am.

XI.

Although it lived till it was grown,
Its fellows it would never own—
Forgetting not the kindness shown
To it by me when left alone.
One day, I turned it out to see
If it would keep the company
Of other lambs—when, instantly,
It left them, running back to me.

XII.

Thus, humanized, it drew content
From those that Nature never meant
To be its partners, when she sent
It in this world where life is spent.
For never, till its dying day,
Did it the full-grown sheep betray;
It was so like sweet Alice Gray,
Its lambhood never passed away.

XIII.

One day, to please the love divine
Of my dear sister Adaline—
Whose spirit now in Heaven doth shine !
I made her, out of new white-pine,

A little waggon with four wheels,
And, harnessing the lamb, with peals
Of laughter ringing at my heels,
I drove her all about the fields.

XIV.

The sheep, with heads uplifted, stared,
As if they thought it were too hard
To be from freedom thus debarred—
Pulling her all about the yard.
Thus did I while the time away
With my dear little Alice Gray—
The little Lamb that lived half way
To Heaven above—the Child of May.

XV.

When it got hungry, as is so
With little lambs on earth below—
I made my little brother go
And steal some bread—his name was JOE.
So, when my joy was most complete,
I called it from the field of wheat;
It ran to me with silver feet,
As if it did its mother meet.

XVI.

And while it stood there by my side,
A rope around its neck I tied,
Expecting soon, with joyful pride,
To take my sister out to ride.
Then, rubbing it upon the head,
Thus to myself I softly said,
" Wait till I get some crumbs of bread"—
When I got back, the lamb was dead !

XVII.

The cord got tangled round its neck
While it was tethered to the stake:
Finding it never more would wake,
I thought my very heart would break!
I buried it deep in the clay,
And went to tell sweet Alice Gray;
The little Lamb that lived half way
To Heaven above—cried all that day.

TO CECILIA.

(Composed on hearing Madame Caradori Allen sing in the Concert Room of the City Hotel, New-York.)

"Thy voice is in my soul !"—*Felicia Hemans.*

I.

The April-shower of thy soft music fell
   Soft on the Summer of my listening ears,
Like Anthems from the lips of Israfel,*
   When all in Heaven are gathered round in tears.

II.

Sweet as the last vibration of those Bells†
   Upon the Trees of God, just as it dies,
Fast by the throne where the Eternal dwells—
   Were the last echoes of thy melodies.

III.

And now thy heavenly beauty steals upon
   My spirit rapt with such divine delight,

---

* "The Angel Israfel, who has the most melodious voice of all God's creatures."—*Sale's Koran.*

† "To these delights will be added the music of golden bells, shaken, as they hang upon the Trees of Eden, by odoriferous winds from the throne of God ; the charms of which will be swollen and diversified by the clashing of the golden-bodied Trees, whose fruits are Pearls and Emeralds."—*Foster's Arabian Nights.*

As when the Moon to young Endymion
Revealed herself in visions of the night.

IV.

Like mellow moonlight in the month of June,
Waning serenely on some far-off sea,
Died the soft pathos of that spiritual tune—
Soft as the liquid hues* of Heaven to me.

* Alluding to the harmony between a soft sound and a blue color.

LORD UTHER'S LAMENT FOR ELLA.

I.

When the milky moon hung crescent,
Like young Grief when Joy is present,
Joy, whose life is evanescent—
   On the horizon's rim, low, low—
From the Vale of Cuscovilla,
Through the Bowers of Boscobella,
Came to meet me Angel-Ella
   In the days of long ago.

II.

By her side Cherubic Aster,
With white limbs like alabaster,
Circled through Heaven's azure pasture,
   Half the fields of night to mow,
When her heart to mine was given—
Then she sang to me at even
Golden melodies of Heaven
   In the days of long ago.

III.

Pure as snow on Himalaya
Was this beautiful bright Baya—*
Bayadere of old Allaya

---

* The Baya is a beautiful bird of Hindostan, about the Sparrow's size,
with yellow-brown, soft plumage, yellow head and feet, with breast

Whom the world could never know;
For within the Boscobella*
Of the Vale of Cuscovilla,†
Died the Sire of Angel-Ella
    In the days of long ago.

IV.

In the mild month of October,
Through the fields of Cooly Rauber,
By the great Archangel Auber,
    Such sweet songs of love did flow,
From her golden lips preluded,
That my soul with joy was flooded,
As by God the earth was wooded
    In the days of long ago.

---

light colored.   In Malabar, it is called the Olimara; in Sanscrit, Bar-
bere ; and in Bengalee, Babiu.   It is a great favorite with the lovers of
Hindostan, who send it forth to pick the jewels from their mistress'
brows.   It is here used as a name of endearment by Lord Uther.

   Boscobella, from two Italian words, signifies beautiful Woods, or
Woodlands.   It was the Eden-wilderness of the Golden Villa of Don
Allaya, whose orchards, which were diversified with all kinds of the
most delicious fruits, were more beautiful than the delightful gardens of
King Alcinous.   His Villa was called Bella Vista, or Beautiful View.   It
was called Golden, because it contained the trophies brought by the
Spanish buccaneers from the Southern seas to old St. Louis' Fort in
Florida, which were recaptured from them when overrun by the savage
myrmidons of the great chiefs from the North.   These treasures, which
consisted of the richest gold and silver plate, corals, pearls, and ermine
of the costliest kind, were bequeathed to Don Allaya by old Lamorah,
the principal chief of the Northern tribes, on his death-bed.   From the
names engraven upon each plate, it was evident that they were the pride
of Spanish Kings.

   † The Vale of Cuscovilla was to the River Mobile what Val-Ombrosa
is to the Arno in Italy.   Cuscovilla was the Holy City of the Southern
tribes.   It was in this valley that Boscobella, the Beautiful Bower of the
villa of Don Allaya, was situated.

V.

All her soul's divinest treasure
Poured she out then without measure,
Till an ocean of deep pleasure
  Drowned my soul from all its wo;
Like Cecilia Inatella,
In the Bowers of Boscobella,
Sang the saintly Angel-Ella
  In the days of long ago.

VI.

In the Violet Valley lying
Dwells the beautiful undying,
While my soul is left here sighing
  That I, too, cannot be so;
For an angel's chariot driven
Through the parting clouds of Heaven,
Bore her soul to God, forgiven
  In the days of long ago.

VII.

Through the shades of Death low looming,
Where the pale night-flowers are blooming,
Goes the brass-winged beetle booming,
  Making silence doubly so;
While my soul is left in sorrow,
Waiting for the bright to-morrow—
Solace none from Hope to borrow—
  For the days of long ago.

VIII.

He who mourns the loved-departed,
Weeps for those who are deserted—
Who in Heaven live broken-hearted
  4*

For the lost left here below;
There, they live in joyful sadness,
Waiting, with exultant madness,
For the left-behind lost gladness
    Of the days of long ago.

IX.

In the Orient Isles of Morning,
Whence there is no more returning,
Thy pure spirit now is burning
    With the stars' serenest glow;
While, as Abraham mourned for Sarah,
By the cypress wells of Marah,*
I now mourn in life's Saharah
    For the days of long ago.

X.

Where the moon hangs never crescent—
(Though she made our nights so pleasant)—
Where God's face is ever present,
    But where tears can never flow;
In the golden Boscobella
Of the Heavenly Cuscovilla
Waits to meet me Angel-Ella,
    As in days of long ago.

XI.

On the green grass, passemented
With the Eden-flowers, sweet scented,
There she sits in Heaven, contented,

---

* Marah means bitterness. When the Israelites came to the Waters
of Marah, in the wilderness of Shur, they could not drink of them be-
cause they were bitter, whereupon Moses " cried unto the Lord, and he
showed him a tree, which, when he had cast it into the waters, the
waters were made sweet."

With the Cherubs on the snow
Of the flowers around them springing—
Angels nectar to them bringing—
Ever shining, ever singing
    Of the days of long ago.

XII.

By her side Cherubic Aster,
With white limbs like alabaster,
Plays along Heaven's emerald pasture—
    Ganymede of joy below—
While her saintly soul sings Pæans
In the Amaranthine Æons
Of high Heaven with her dear Fleance,
    Of the days of long ago.

XIII.

Soon my sighing soul shall follow
Her from this dark grave we hallow,
Up to God's Divine Valhalla,
    There to sing forever mo
In the Bowers of Chalcedony
Of the Heavenly Avalona,*
With the plaintive voice of Cona,†
    Of the days of long ago.

---

* The Vale of Avalon, where King Arthur, the son of Uther, was wounded. It was the valley of the pausing of the Moon.

† Cona—one of the most beautiful of the female characters of Ossian.

TO MARY IN HEAVEN.

I.

I met thee first in May, Mary!
  The flower-crowned month of May;
But now thou art away, Mary!
  Away from me—away!
Thou wert that all to me, Mary!
  That all on earth to me,
That I will be to thee, Mary!
  In Heaven above to thee.

II.

Ah! then thine eyes were mild, Mary!
  Thy deep blue eyes were mild;
For thou wert then a child, Mary!
  And I another child.
Thou wert that all to me, Mary!
  That all on earth to me,
That I will be to thee, Mary!
  In Heaven above to thee.

III.

Thy face was then so meek, Mary!
  So saintly mild, so meek,
Thy lily-form seemed weak, Mary!
  And mine for thine grew weak

For thou wert that to me, Mary!
　That all on earth to me,
That I will be to thee, Mary!
　In Heaven above to thee.

IV.

You led me through the meads, Mary!
　The flower-enameled meads,
By brooks of rustling reeds, Mary!
　By brooks of rustling reeds—
Where thou wert that to me, Mary!
　That all on earth to me,
That I will be to thee, Mary!
　In Heaven above to thee.

V.

Wherever you then went, Mary!
　No matter where you went—
I followed with content, Mary!
　Because you were content.
For thou wert that to me, Mary!
　That all on earth to me,
That I will be to thee, Mary!
　In Heaven above to thee.

VI.

I recollect the morn, Mary!
　The beautiful May-Morn,
Beside the Field of Corn, Mary!
　The rustling reeds of Corn—
That thou wert that to me, Mary!
　That all on earth to me,
That I will be to thee, Mary!
　In Heaven above to thee.

VII.

Ah! then I took thy hand, Mary!
  Thy lily snow-white hand;
And walked along the sand, Mary!
  The milk-white road of sand.
For thou wert that to me, Mary!
  That all on earth to me,
That I will be to thee, Mary!
  In Heaven above to thee.

VIII.

I caught thee round the waist, Mary!
  The slender Sylph-like waist,
And felt my heart beat fast, Mary!
  Because thine own beat fast.
For thou wert that to me, Mary!
  That all on earth to me,
That I will be to thee, Mary!
  In Heaven above to thee.

IX.

Such words fell from thy tongue, Mary!
  Such sweet words from thy tongue,
That when you talked you sung, Mary!
  You never talked but sung.
Then thou wert that to me, Mary!
  That all on earth to me,
That I will be to thee, Mary!
  In Heaven above to thee.

X.

Thus through the month of May, Mary!
  The flower-crowned month of May,
We, courting, went to play, Mary!
  And courted in our play.

The years were then to me, Mary !
　As hours are now to me ;
As time is now to thee, Mary !
　In Heaven above to thee.

XI.

For Love knows nought of years, Mary !
　Love nothing knows of years ;
And sheds no bitter tears, Mary !
　Time measured is by tears.
Thus thou wert that to me, Mary !
　That all on earth to me,
That I will be to thee, Mary !
　In Heaven above to thee.

XII.

What thou art now above, Mary !
　I was, as if above ;
For Heaven is made of love, Mary !
　And I was full of love.
For thou wert that to me, Mary !
　That all on earth to me,
That I will be to thee, Mary !
　In Heaven above to thee.

XIII.

But now these days are gone, Mary !
　These HALCYON DAYS are gone !
And I am left alone, Mary !
　Alone on earth—alone !
What would I give to see, Mary !
　Thy precious form to see ?
All thou wouldst give to be, Mary !
　In this dark world with me.

THE SHELL.

" It seems in truth the fairest shell of ocean."—SHELLEY.

I.

What is it makes thy sound unto my ear
  So mournful, Angel of the mighty Sea?
Is it the soul of her who once was here,
  Speaking affection, through thy lips, to me?

II.

Oh! from my childhood this has been to me
  A mystery which no one could solve!—It sounds
And sorrows for the Sea incessantly—
  Telling the grief with which my soul abounds!

III.

Here, in its labyrinthine curve, it leaves
  The foot-prints of its song in many dyes;
And here, incessantly, it ever weaves
  The rainbow-tissue of its melodies.

IV.

When any harsher sound disturbs me here,
  In my lamentings in this world for thee,
I will apply it to my listening ear,
  And think it is thy soul come down to me.

THE DYING SWAN.

I.

Fair as the crescent Moon supine in Heaven,
  Floating among the Reeds which seemed to love her,
Beneath an emerald Willow, late at even,
  Weeping upon the River just above her—
  As if the soul within was music that did move her—

II.

A virgin Swan came in the time of Spring,
  Wrapped in the winding-sheet of her own whiteness—
Her Heaven-revealing dying Song to sing—
  Breasting the stream with such majestic brightness
  It seemed awe-struck beneath her bosom's downy lightness.

III.

The cataract of her song, at first, was mild,
  But like Ezekiel's River, wider growing,
Till all the world became an ocean wild—
  It gathered volume with its onward flowing—
  As if *her* joy sprung from the bliss she was bestowing.

IV.

As if some Angel down from Heaven had come
  To sing the GREAT DAY of the Resurrection,
When all the thunder-cataracts grew dumb
  At his loud Gabriel-voice—by God's direction,
  Opening the graves for Man to rise in every section—

V.

Like that great Amphionic-Song of joy,
　　Whose Mountain-moving, Titan-jubilations
Built up, impregnable, the walls of Troy—
　　Giving to stones the heart's divine pulsations—　　[tions—
　　While teaching Heaven's world-making tongue unto the Na-

VI.

Her mighty, soul-uplifting melody—
　　Strong as an Angel's wing rising to glory
With the redeemed who died in purity—
　　Shouting to Angels at Heaven's Gate the story
　　Of her release from Earth where she had long been sorry—

VII.

In clarion-shouts of blissful joyance sprung
　　Out of her heart in whirlwind-jubilations—
Rising in fiery swiftness from her tongue,
　　In wild, Elysian chant—as when two Nations,
　　Like clouds do thunder, lift their Heavenward acclamations

VIII.

In Hallelujah-shouts for Liberty's dear sake—
　　Upsent out of each lightning-soul in thunder—
As if each mighty, Titan-heart would break
　　With its great earthquake-joy—tearing asunder
　　The Tyrant's throne—mute now with supernatural wonder !

IX.

Till all the golden-tongued Pierides
　　Upon the Olympian Mountain loudly singing—
Filling Thessalia's Vale with music to the seas,
　　Whose storm-uplifted billows now were flinging
　　Their tribute of rare shells upon the shore, upspringing—

X.

Were hushed to silence mute as hungry Death
   When listening for the footsteps of the Living ;
Till great Poseidon held his mighty breath,
     The tribute of rare audience mutely giving—
     Proclaiming, louder than in storms, the joy he was receiving.

XI.

This Niobe of Birds, rapt in Apocalypse,
   Deluged the world with her Seraphic wailing—
Turning the Stars in Heaven to an eclipse—
     (Her joy, at length, above her grief prevailing—)
     Proving that all except Grief's Song for grief is unavailing.

XII.

Thus did her soul pour forth its song's deep meer,
   In emulation of the God-like thunder
Of Saturn-overturning Jupiter,
     Whose Heaven-usurping vengeance took with wonder
     The Immortal Gods—tearing their Ramparts all asunder !

XIII.

Like some impetuous River to the Sea,
   Greening the Vallies through which it goes rolling,
With vital freshness—her sweet melody,
     In crystal, joy-creating, grief-controlling   [soling.
     Volume, poured through all the thirsting world its cool con-

XIV.

Then, as some Dove-like Soul on wings of fire—
   (Forced from her husband twice on earth to sever—)
In blazing Chariot from her funeral pyre,
     Ascends to Heaven unscathed, rejoicing ever—
     All purified, redeemed from mortal taint forever—

XV.

Swift rising on the circling wings of song,
   Out of her burning heart in transport soaring—
Leaving the Harp vibrating of her tongue—
   So rose her soul—(all other souls restoring—)
   Up to the God in Heaven she died on earth adoring.

XVI.

The cloud-sustaining, many-folded Hills—
   The soft, retiring mystery of the Vallies—
The open frankness of the verdant Fields—
   The winding labyrinths of the emerald Alleys—
   The bending Heavens, with all the Stars in cyclic sallies—

XVII.

The open mouths of Mountains—the dim Caves—
   Echoed her music with reverberant thunder,
From their sepulchral throats—deep as the grave's—
   Dying around Night's throne now torn asunder—
   Leaving the rapt World mute with supernatural wonder!—

XVIII.

This was the Gospel taught by that rapt SWAN—
   White Angel-Prophet on the waters dying!
That many pleasures in this world foregone,
   Are but the works of our great Faith relying
   On Heaven for good, for which we are forever sighing.

XIX.

This was the great EVANGEL of that SWAN—
   That *not* on Earth is that UNFADING TREASURE
For which we yearn as Night does for the Dawn;
   But after death we shall possess the pleasure
   Which God in Heaven has laid up for us without measure.

ISADORE.

" I approach thee—I look dauntless into thine eyes. The soul that loves can dare
all things. Shadow, I defy thee, and compel."—*Zanoni.*

I.

While the world lay round me sleeping,
   I, alone, for ISADORE,
Patient Vigils lonely keeping—
Some one said to me while weeping,
   " Why this grief forever more ?"
And I answered, " I am weeping
   For my blessed ISADORE !"

II.

Then the VOICE again said, " Never
   Shall thy soul see ISADORE !
God from thee thy love did sever—
He has damned thy soul forever !
   Wherefore then her loss deplore ?
Thou shalt live in Hell forever !
   Heaven now holds thine ISADORE !

III.

" She is dead—the world benighted—
   Dark for want of ISADORE !
Have not all your hopes been blighted ?
How can you be reunited ?

Can mere words the dead restore ?
Have not all your hopes been blighted ?
Why then hope for ISADORE ?"

IV.

"Back to Hell, thou ghostly Horror !"
Thus I cried, dear ISADORE !
" Phantom of remorseless Sorrow !
Death might from thee palor borrow—
Borrow leanness ever more !
Back to Hell again !—to-morrow
I will go to ISADORE !"

V.

" When my soul to Heaven is taken,"
Were thy words, dear ISADORE !
" Let no other one awaken
In thy heart, because forsaken,
What was felt for me before !
When my soul to Heaven is taken,
Oh ! forget not ISADORE !

VI.

" Oh ! remember this, Politian !"
Said my dying ISADORE !
" Till from out this clayey prison
In the flowery FIELDS ELYSIAN
We unite forever more !
Oh ! remember this, Politian !
And forget not ISADORE !"

VII.

Then before my raptured vision
Came sweet HOPE, dear ISADORE !
From the flowery FIELDS ELYSIAN,

Crying out to me, " Politian !
Rise—rejoice forever more !
Angels wait for thee, Politian !
Up to Heaven to ISADORE !"

VIII.

Then from out my soul departed
Deepest grief, dear ISADORE !
Bliss, that never me deserted,
Entered in the broken-hearted—
Giving life forever more—
Bliss that never me deserted,
Like thy love, dear ISADORE !

IX.

Myriad VOICES still are crying,
Day and night, dear ISADORE !
"Come, come to the PURE LAND* lying
Far up in the sky undying—
There to rest forever more !
Purified, redeemed, undying—
Come to Heaven to ISADORE !

---

* Plato speaks of the " PURE EARTH" above, (την γην χαθαραν εν χαθαρω
χεισθαι ουρανο,) the abode of Divinity, of innocence, and life. It is an im-
memorial tradition. It was a revelation to the Hebrews. This " PURE
EARTH" above, is, no doubt, the primeval Paradise of Love—the ante-
type of that which Adam lost. Aristotle, in his Hymn to Virtue, speaks
of the " BLESSED ISLES" above. The Νησοι Μακάρων, or ISLES OF THE
BLEST, were the ELYSIUM of the departed Heroes who were considered
immortal—the same as the MANITOLINE of the Indians, where they say
the souls of the deathless Chieftains of the world dance in hormonian
choirs around the throne of Ataensic to the most delightful music.
They believe that the future felicity of the departed of this world consists
in rejoining, in the flower-gemmed Savannahs of the Fields of Immor-
tality, the long lost objects of their affections in the joyful festivities of
the Chase.

X.

"Blest Companion of th' Eternal !
    Come away to ISADORE !
From the griefs that are diurnal
To the joys that are supernal—
    Sempiternal on Heaven's shore !
Bliss supernal, joys eternal
    Up in Heaven with ISADORE.

XI.

"Cast away thy garb of mourning,
    Worn so long for ISADORE !
For those glory-garments burning
In the BRIGHT ISLES OF THE MORNING,
    Like the stars forever more.
Golden Days are now returning—
    Up to Heaven to ISADORE !

XII.

"Lay aside thy load of sorrow,
    Borne so long for ISADORE !
Pilgrim, pierced by Death's cold arrow,
Thou shalt see thy love to-morrow
    Up in Heaven forever more !
Lay aside thy load of sorrow—
    Come to Heaven to ISADORE !

XIII.

"Come away, Oh ! mournful mortal !
    Come to Heaven to ISADORE !
Through Death's ebon, iron Portal
To the joys that are immortal
    On Helusion's happy shore !
Come away, Oh ! mournful mortal !
    Into Heaven to ISADORE !

XIV.

" Up to God who will befriend you !
　Up to Heaven to ISADORE !
Angels waiting to attend you—
Every aid you wish to lend you—
　Singing, shouting on Heaven's shore !
Angels waiting to attend you
　To your blessed ISADORE !"

XV.

From the griefs that are diurnal—
　Bitter griefs, dear ISADORE !
To the joys that are eternal—
To the bliss that is supernal—
　Sempiternal on Heaven's shore—
Thou art gone through years eternal
　There to rest, dear ISADORE !

XVI.

There they comates shall be Angels—
　White-robed Angels, ISADORE !
Singing Heaven's DIVINE EVANGELS
Through the Eternal Years, all change else,
　Changeless there forever more !
Thou, ASTRATE of the Angels !
　Knowest this so, dear ISADORE !

XVII.

From the Paradise now wasted
　Of thy form, dear ISADORE !
Lilly-bell that Death has blasted !
Purest Pleasures have I tasted
　In the Edenic days of Yore.
Joys celestial have I tasted
　From thy flower, dear ISADORE !

5

XVIII.

Like two spirits in one being,
    Were our souls, dear ISADORE!
Every object singly seeing—
In all things, like one, agreeing
    In those HALCYON DAYS of Yore.
We shall live so in our being
    Up in Heaven, dear ISADORE!

XIX.

Myriad Voices still are crying
    Day and night, dear ISADORE!
" Come, come to the PURE LAND lying
Far up in the sky undying—
    There to rest forever more!
Purified, redeemed, undying—
    Come to Heaven to ISADORE!

XX.

ADON-AI! GOD OF GLORY!
    Who dost love mine ISADORE!
Who didst hear her prayerful story
In this world when she was sorry—
    Gone to Heaven forever more!
ADON-AI! GOD OF GLORY!
    Take me home to ISADORE!

THE GOSPEL OF LOVE.

"Heaven lies about us in our infancy."—*Wordsworth.*

"He that will humble himself to go to a child for instruction, will come away a wiser and a better man. Better to be driven out from among men, than to be disliked of children."—*Charles H. Dana.*

I.

You beat the child into distress,
That you may force him to confess
His faults—then, penitent, caress
His penitential bitterness.

II.

You force from out his heart the tears
That have been sleeping there for years,
By waking not his love but fears—
He only thus reformed appears.

III.

For your own heart's offended sake,
Him to your arms again you take—
Keeping his former love awake ;
Else, like his own, *your* heart would break !

IV.

But had you not caressed the child,
Thereby becoming reconciled

To him, now he is so exiled—
You had not tamed, but made more wild.

v.

It was your kindness was the cure,
And not the pain he did endure ;
Else why the after-overture
His former friendship to secure ?

vi.

To punish one that does not need
The punishment, is to exceed
His guilt, did he deserve to bleed,
By doing far the greater deed.

vii.

No evil underneath the sun
Is greater than this very one ;
What tenderness at first had done,
Makes after-overture just none.

viii.

Why should you first withdraw your love
To punish him ? then, after, prove,
By kindness, what it did behoove
You first to do his heart to move ?

ix.

Your after-kindness only shows
That what you tried to do by blows,
(Which your own heart, now melted, knows,)
From acts of kindness only flows.

X.

Thus what you try by force to bend
You only break—this is its end ;
By forcing Nature to contend,
You only mar what you would mend.

XI.

What Nature says is right, *is* so :
This every man on earth should know,
That, feeling for another's wo,
Is what we all were born to do.

XII.

To make the Man, build up the child—
Still keeping pure the undefiled ;
To tame is not to make more wild :
This must be done by acts most mild.

XIII.

That doth the father's heart defile
Which makes him to his child hostile ;
The vigor born of such black bile,
Is evidence itself of guile.

XIV.

Healing the blow, that caused him pain,
By after-kindness, proves it vain ;
For that which will not him restrain,
Helps him to do the deed again.

XV.

The child's soul must be first imbued
With principles of perfect good,
Before it can be thus renewed
To walk the path of rectitude

XVI.

The madness we can not endure,
We send to Hospitals to cure—
Purging the heart to make it pure,
From future ills to keep secure.

XVII.

A fostering kindness is the way
To purge such darkness all away
From that poor soul now led astray—
Letting in TRUTH's eternal Day.

XVIII.

This law unto the soul was given
When God first sent it down from Heaven—
By force no heart is bent—but riven :
Man may be led—but *never* driven.

XIX.

That which belongs alone to God,
He has upon no man bestowed ;
Death-punishment, therefore, for good,
Should be erased from penal code.

THE GREAT REFORMER

I.

Like the holy men of Tabor,
    Bloody sweat upon his brow—
Here he travailed long in labor—
    His reward is with him now.

II.

With sublime, divine uprightness,
    By the lightning of his thought,
Like an Angel's sword in brightness
    Was the World's great battle fought.

III.

Fired with Prophet-inspiration,
    Words of lightning fiercely fell
From his lips of Jubilation—
    Withering up the hosts of Hell!

IV.

Full of God's eternal Spirit,
    Gospel-charmed, the spirit's spell,
Preaching TRUTH, he did inherit
    Heaven on earth instead of Hell.

V.

Thus did he fulfil his Mission,
　　Making Earth like Heaven above—
Healing, like the Great Physician,
　　Human hearts with heavenly love.

VI.

So his soul's Divine Hosanna
　　Cheered Earth's children in distress,
As Heaven rained on Israel manna,
　　Journeying through the wilderness.

VII.

For his soul's Divine Evangels
　　Fell so sweetly from his tongue,
That his speech seemed like an Angel's,
　　As if he in Heaven had Sung.

VIII.

Flower-enameled, golden-sanded
　　Was the path on which he trod
From the Pearl-shore, where he landed,
　　To the holy House of God.

EVENING.

I.

Out of the crystal Gates of Heaven,
Now comes the pensive blue-eyed Even,
Weeping like Eve, when first forgiven
In penitence, from Eden driven.

II.

Down in the acromatic streams,
Meeting the luminiferous beams
With which the air forever teems,
The golden mail of minnows gleams.

III.

Up from the blade-embattled banks
Of the cool stream, the deer, in ranks,
Are going now to give God thanks,
By playing on the hills their pranks.

IV.

Over the Pastures green the lambs
Go bleating round their snowy dams—
Drawing sweet comfort from the calms
Along the hillside by the rams.

5*

V.

The Ring-dove coos her woodnotes wild,
As artless as an innocent child—
Drawing her bliss from undefiled
Connubial truth in meekness mild.

VI.

The budding Lily yields her heart
The Summer Sun now to dispart ;
A saintly virgin void of art,
Joy to all Nature to impart.

VII.

Impearled in drops of beaded dew,
The Violet opes her eye of blue,
The pensive Nun in Heaven to view,
So early crescent, born anew.

VIII.

Out of the red heart of the rose
A liquid honey softly flows—
The Atter-gul made as she grows—
Condensed in nectar as she blows.

IX.

The white Swans, in the rustling Reeds,
Clamor with joy, as in the weeds
The matron builds the nest she needs,
While her mute mate around her feeds.

X.

The Red-Bird, with his coral crest,
Carols aloud from out his breast,
While nigh, his mate, supremely blest,
Among the branches, builds her nest.

KYRIE ELEISON.

"De profundis clamavi ad te Domine."

I.

By the Heaven-revealing STRANGER
Nursed by Mary in the Manger
To preserve him from all danger—
    Kyrie Eleison !*

II.

By the TRUTHS that he came teaching,
Which the Apostles died in preaching—
Heaven the sooner for it reaching—
    Kyrie Eleison !

III.

By the comfort still proceeding
From his Words, that all are needing,
When our hearts within are bleeding—
    Kyrie Eleison!

IV.

By the Heaven-eclipsing anguish
That he suffered, Hell to vanquish,
On the cross where he did languish—
    Kyrie Eleison !

---

* Lord, have mercy.

v.

By his body torn asunder,
When his lightning-groans in thunder
Struck the Angels dumb with wonder—
                    Kyrie Eleison!

vi.

By his golden voice when crying,
" IT IS FINISHED !"—(God replying
In an earthquake)—fainting—dying—
                    Kyrie Eleison!

vii.

By his bounteous Benediction
Breathed on earth for our affliction
At his glorious resurrection—
                    Kyrie Eleison!

viii.

By this LORD OF LIGHT returning
Back to Heaven, with glory burning
In the BRIGHT ISLES OF THE MORNING—
                    Kyrie Eleison!

ix.

By the Fountains Everlasting—
Ever flowing—never wasting—
His pure spirit now is tasting—
                    Kyrie Eleison!

x.

By the death that Stephen suffered,
When his soul to God was offered—
Gift like that which Peter proffered—
                    Kyrie Eleison!

XI.

By his soul-uplifting story,
Which to read now makes me sorry,—
How he "fell asleep" in glory—
            Kyrie Eleison !

XII.

By the DAY-SPRING on him breaking,
From the sweet sleep he was taking
By the GATES OF GOD, when waking—
            Kyrie Eleison !

XIII.

By the earnest expectation
Of the glorious consummation
Of our hopes in Heaven's salvation—
            Kyrie Eleison !

XIV.

By the faith of childless Hannah—
Wife of Shiloh-loved Elkanah—
(As to Israel Christ gave Manna—)
            Kyrie Eleison !

XV.

By his bounteous BENEDICTUS
Breathed in Heaven for our delectus—
AGNUS DEI to direct us—
            Kyrie Eleison !

XVI.

By the words that he has spoken—
Vows that never can be broken—
Of our joys in Heaven the token—
            KYRIE ELEISON !

BURDENS OF UNREST.

—

MARY'S LAMENT FOR SHELLEY LOST AT SEA.

" *Stay for me there !* I will not fail
To meet thee in that hollow vale !"—*Bishop Henry King*

—

" Thou wilt not be consoled—I wonder not !"—*Shelley.*

—

I.

I HEAR thy spirit calling unto me
   From out the deep,
Like Archytas* from old Venetia's sea,
   While I here weep !
Saying, Come, strew my body with the sand,
And bury me upon the land, the land—
Out of this sea, dear Mary ! on the land, the land !

II.

Oh ! never, never more ! no, never more !
   Lost in the deep !
Will thy sweet beauty visit this dark shore,
   Where I now weep !
For thou art gone forevermore from me,
Sweet Mariner ! lost, murdered by the sea!
Ulysses of my soul's deep love lost in the sea !

---

* " Horace represents the spirit of Archytas addressing itself, from the Gulf of Venice, to a Mariner, earnestly requesting him to strew light sand over his body, which lay unburied on the beach."—*Buck's Beauties and Sublimities of Nature.*

III.

Ever—forevermore, bright, glorious one,
　　Drowned in the deep !
In Spring-time—Summer—Winter—all alone—
　　Must I here weep !
Thou spirit of my soul ! thou light of life !
While thou art absent, Shelley, from thy wife !
Absent, dear Swan of Albion, from thy weeping wife !

IV.

Celestial pleasure once to contemplate
　　Thy power, great Deep !
Possest my soul ! but evermore shall hate,
　　While I here weep !
Crowd out thy memory from my soul, oh ! Sea !
For killing him who was so dear to me !
More dear than Heaven's high Lord to Mary unto me !

V

He was the incarnation of pure Truth,
　　Oh ! mighty Deep !
And thou didst murder him in prime of youth,
　　For whom I weep !
And, murdering him, didst *more* than murder me !
Who was my Heaven on earth, oh ! treacherous Sea !
My *more* than Heaven on earth, oh ! *more* than murderous Sea !

VI.

My spirit wearied not to succor his,
　　Oh ! mighty Deep !
The oftener done the greater was the bliss ;
　　But now I weep !
And where his beauty lay, unceasing pain
Now dwells—my heart can know no joy again !
Poor Doveless Ark ! can know no joy on earth again !

VII.

God of my fathers! God of that bright One
        Drowned in the Deep!
Shall we not meet again beyond the sun—
        No more to weep?
Yes, I shall meet him there—the lost—the bright—
The glorious Shelley! Spring of my delight!
Fountain of all my pleasure! life of my delight!

VIII.

Now, like Orion on some cloudless night
        Above the Deep,
I see his soul look down from Heaven—*how bright!*
        While I here weep!
And there, like Hesperus the stars of even,
Beckon my soul away to him in Heaven—
Sitting, star-crowned, upon the highest sill in Heaven!

THE CHAPLET OF CYPRESS.

AN ELEGY ON THE DEATH OF MY SISTER.

" The Good die first."

I.

Up through the hyaline ether-sea,
Star-diademed, in chariot of pure pain,
 Through th' empyreal star-fires radiantly,
Triumphant over Death in Heaven to reign
  Thy soul is gone, seeking its BLEST ABODE,
  Where break the songs of stars against the feet of God.

II.

At Heaven's high portals thou dost stand,
Bands of attendant Angels by thy side—
 Gazing with rapture on the PROMISED LAND—
Pale—meek—with thy last sickness, purified,
  By suffering, from the sins of earth, to be
  A white-robed Angel round God's throne eternally.

III.

Like stars at midnight in the sky,
Were all the dark things in this world to thee;
 The joys of earth, when thou wert called to die,
Were ringing in thine ears most audibly,
  When Angel-voices from the far-off skies,
  Poured on thy soul rivers of rapturous melodies

IV.

Upon thy pale, cold, silent face,
Still speaking of the death that thou didst die—
  A living light, which Death could not efface,
Was shed, crowning thy young mortality—
  As if the power had unto thee been given
  To show us here on earth what thou art now in Heaven.

V.

For when thy coffin-lid was moved,
Fast flowing tears of endless pity fell
  Upon thy pale, cold brow, so much beloved,
From our torn hearts, as we then cried, FAREWELL!
  Like dews upon some withered lily-leaf—
  Rivers of sorrow from deep seas of bitter grief!

VI.

At thine, the newest grave dug here,
Beside our parents' graves, we humbly bow,
  Offering our hearts to God in silent prayer—
Asking ourselves who of us next must go
  Where thou art gone, to see what thou hast seen—
  To be what thou art now, if now what thou hast been!

VII.

I recollect the last long night
We played together—brothers—sisters—all—
  Took notice of the infinite delight
That filled thy soul, till laughter's waterfall
  Gushed, gurgling from thy lips in joyful flow—
  And this, dear ONE! was only three short months ago!

VIII.

Then thou wert gayer than the gay,
And full of pleasure to the very brim—
  Whiling, with gladness, all thy time away—
Not thinking thou wert soon to go to HIM—
  Thy Father's father, there, in Heaven, to shine
  With thy dear mother—brother—sister Adaline!

IX.

Thou wilt behold my Florence there,
And she will know thee in that world above,
  By that, which, wanting, makes us strangers here!
And she will love thee with the same deep love
  She loved me in this world, if thou wilt tell
  Her thou art my dear sister—Angel! fare-thee-well!

THRENODY.

COMPOSED ON THE DEATH OF MY LITTLE BOY.

"I will complain in the bitterness of my soul."—*Job*, vii. 11.

I.

By the Waters of Salvation,
    Christ's Salvation, full of pain—
Christ's Salvation, in probation,
I sit down in tribulation,
And now write this Lamentation
    For the lost, the early slain!
Waiting, (hoping for salvation,)
    For his coming back again.

II.

Ah! Angelic was my Tommy,
    Tommy, Death has early slain,
Tommy taken early from me!
Whose sweet life did so become me,
That his death doth now consume me—
    Parching up my heart with pain!
Ah! Angelic was my Tommy—
    Never coming back again!

III.

How I miss him in the summer,
    Summer of the Golden Grain—
Summer, when the dove doth murmur
For the mate that is torn from her—

Sighing out to each new comer
  All her heart's melodious pain !
Waiting all the livelong summer
  For his coming back again !

IV.

Early frosted Flower of Aiden,
  Aiden where there is no pain—
Aiden where the soul lives laden
With the joys that are unfaden—
Saintly Lily, infant maiden,
  Ada of my heart of pain !
Thou art with him now in Aiden—
  Never coming back again !

V.

Like the glorified Orion,
  Blest Orion who was slain !
Bright Orion who lives high on
High Eternity's Mount Zion—
So my little Christ did die on
  This dark Calvary of pain !
Like the glorified Orion—
  Never coming back again !

VI.

In that undefiled bright Thule,
  Thule of eternal gain—
Thule were the soul sees newly
From the Isles of Inatula
To the golden bowered Beula,
  Where his Saviour Christ doth reign ;
In that undefiled bright Thule—
  Never coming back again !

VII.

All my days are spent in weeping,
   Weeping for the early slain—
Weeping, patient vigils keeping
By the grave where he is sleeping,
Sorrow from Death's field still reaping
   Reaping for the early slain !
All my days are spent in weeping
   For his coming back again !

VIII.

On the earth are now no traces,
   Traces of his former reign—
Traces, where the joyful faces
Of his sisters, like the Graces,
Made an Eden of the places
   Where they met in my domain ;
On the earth are now no traces
   Of his coming back again !

IX.

I shall never more see Pleasure,
   Pleasure never more, but pain—
Pleasure, losing that dear treasure
Whom I loved here without measure,
Whose sweet eyes were Heaven's own azure,
   Sparkling, mild, like sunny rain !
I shall never more see Pleasure
   For his coming back again !

X.

How my weary soul doth miss him,
   Miss him here in bitter pain—
Miss him when I want to kiss him,
At the night when I should bless him,

When his mother should undress him
  For the bed where he has lain !
How my soul doth always miss him—
  Never coming back again !

XI.

How we miss his songs of gladness,
  Gladness far too deep for pain—
Gladness too divine for sadness,
Poured with such exultant madness
That it seemed just done for badness,
  As in sunshine falls the rain ;
All my soul is turned to sadness
  For his coming back again !

XII.

How my soul doth long to meet him,
  Meet him in this world again—
Meet him where I used to greet him,
As the Saints in Heaven now treat him—
On my vacant knees to seat him,
  Where in joy he used to reign ;
How my soul doth long to meet him
  In this trying world again !

XIII.

Where the nightingale sits singing,
  Singing with impassioned pain—
Singing, while the Heavens are ringing
With his river-song upspringing—
Into Heaven his soul went winging
  Of its way with Christ to reign ;
There my little Bird sits singing—
  Never coming back again !

XIV.

All my tears are unavailing,
　Unavailing all this pain—
Unavailing all this wailing
Of my heart that now is failing
With its weight of wo, unveiling
　All my soul's deep grief in vain!
All my sighs are unavailing—
　He will never come again!

XV.

Soon my sighing soul, death-blighted,
　Blighted, racked with bitter pain—
Blighted, burthened, all benighted,
Shall in Heaven above be righted,
Glorified, redeemed, requited,
　When it meets my early slain;
There to wait no more death-blighted,
　For his coming back again.

XVI.

Hang thy harp upon the willow,
　Willow weeping tears of rain—
Willow shading the soft billow
Of his grave with light so mellow,
Just above the satin pillow
　Where his head so long has lain!
Hang thy harp upon the willow—
　He will never come again!

XVII.

Ah! when shall I ever hold him,
  Hold him in these arms again?
Hold him, tenderly enfold him,
And with tears of joy behold him,
And retell what I have told him—
  Kissing him with joyful pain!—
Up in Heaven I shall behold him—
  I shall meet him there again.

THE VIOLET IN THE VALLEY OF DEATH.

AN ELEGY ON THE DEATH OF MY LITTLE CHILD.

When Solon wept for the death of his son, some one said, " Weeping will not help."
He answered, "Alas! therefore, I weep, because weeping will not help!"

I.

Hushed is now thy bitter crying,
   Folded in the calm serene
Of the peace of God undying,
   Beautiful divine Eugene!
For thy soul ascends, returning
   Back to Heaven where it was born,
With Beatus in it burning
   For the Everlasting Morn.
May the Lord in Heaven have mercy
   On thy soul, my darling child!
Precious blue-eyed Eugene Percy!
   Blessed babe that never smiled!

II.

Tenderest tears of sorrow ever
   From my heart's deep fount shall flow,
Watering Love's sweet flower forever,
   Which by tears can only grow.
Losing that divinest treasure
   God in Heaven had given to me,
Nothing now can give me pleasure,
   But the Hopes of meeting thee.

May the Lord in Heaven have mercy
On thy soul, my darling child!
Precious blue-eyed Eugene Percy!
Blessed babe that never smiled!

III.

Like the Moon in her own splendor,
   Waning on some cloudless night,
Lay thy lily-limbs so tender,
   Shrouded in their own pure light
Now thy blessed star-like spirit,
   Glory-circled, full of love,
Doth the joys of Heaven inherit,
   Cradled in Christ's breast above.
Thus the Lord of Heaven has mercy
On thy soul, my darling child!
Precious blue-eyed Eugene Percy!
Blessed babe that never smiled!

IV.

From the Fountains Everlasting,
   Flowing out of God's great store,
Thy pure spirit now is tasting
   Bliss divine forever more.
In the golden sunny silence
   Of the bliss of God serene—
Young Dove of the Blessed Islands
   Liveth my divine Eugene.
Thus the Lord in Heaven has mercy
On thy soul, my darling child!
Precious blue-eyed Eugene Percy!
Blessed babe that never smiled!

V.

Underneath the saintly roses
   Blooming round me while I weep,
Near where Florence now reposes—
   Take thy fill of peaceful sleep.
Silent on thy satin pillow
   Rest thy pensive little head,
While above the weeping willow
   Tells my sorrows for the dead!
For the Lord in Heaven has mercy
   On thy soul, my darling child!
Precious blue-eyed Eugene Percy!
   Blessed babe that never smiled!

TO ISA IN HEAVEN.

"EARLY, bright, transient. chaste as morning dew.
She sparkled. was exhaled and went to heaven !"—*Young.*

I.

Where is she now?
Oh! Isa! tell me where thou art?
If Death has laid his hand upon thy brow,
   Has he not touched my heart?
Has he not laid it in the grave with thine,
And buried all my joys?—Speak! thou art mine!

II.

If thou wert dead,
I would not ask thee to reply;
But thou art living—thy dear soul has fled
   To Heaven where it can never die!
Then why not come to me? Return—return,
And comfort me, for I have much to mourn!

III.

I sigh all day!
I mourn for thee the livelong night!
And when the next night comes, thou art away,
   And so is absent my delight!
Oh! as the lone dove for his absent mate,
So is my soul for thee disconsolate!

IV.

I long for death—
For any thing—to be with thee !
I did inhale, alas ! thy dying breath,
That it might have some power on me
To make me what thou art !—but, thou art dead !
And I am here !—it strengthened me instead !

V.

Joy there is none—
It went into the grave with thee !
And Grief, because my spirit is alone,
Is all that comes to comfort me !
The very air I breathe is turned to sighs,
And all my soul seems melting from mine eyes.

VI.

I hear, at even,
The liquid carol of the birds ;
Their music makes me think of thee in Heaven,
It is so much like thy sweet words.
The brooklet whispers, as it runs along,
Our first love-story with its liquid tongue.

VII.

Wake, Isa ! wake !
And come back in this world again !
Oh ! come down to me, for my soul's dear sake,
And cure me of this trying pain !
I would give all that earth to man can be,
If thou wert only in this world with me !

VIII.

Day after day
I seek thee, but thou art not near!
I sit down by thy grave in the cold clay,
And listen for thy soul!—oh! dear!
And when some withered leaf falls from the tree,
I start, as if thy soul had spoke to me!

IX.

And so it is,
And so it evermore must be
To him, who has been robbed of all the bliss
He ever knew, by losing thee!
For Misery, in thine absence, is my wife!
What Joy had been, hadst thou remained in life!

X.

It is now even!
The birds have sung themselves to sleep;
And all the stars seem coming out of Heaven,
As if to look upon me weep!—
Oh! let me not look up to thee in vain,
But come back to me in this world again!

THE CROSS OF MY CROWN.

I.

If thou wert dead I would not weep,
  For then my spirit soon would be
Free from this sorrow which now makes me keep
  Such vigils of deep agony
  Forever more for thee.

II.

I once did think, in my deep love,
  That thou wert never born to die ;
But came down solely from the Heavens above
  To live with me eternally,
  As thou didst live on high.

III.

But since thou hast been false to me,
  I know that thou wert born to die ;
For wanting that sweet Heavenly purity
  The Angels have in Heaven on high—
  Doth breed mortality !

IV.

I sigh for thee the livelong day—
  I mourn for thee the long, long night !
For Heaven thus absent from my soul alway,
  Shuts out forever from my sight
  My heart's divine delight !

v.

Thou wert the world wherein I dwelt—
　Lost now since thou art gone from me !
The only Heaven to which my spirit knelt,
　And worshiped, weeping, wonderingly—
　Finding my God in thee !

vi.

But now—since thou art false to me—
　I am of mine own soul afraid !
For if the Angel that once dwelt in thee,
　Was Hell in Heaven's own light arrayed—
　What may not Heaven be made ?

vii.

If thou wert all this world to me,
　What have I now since thou art gone ?
But worldless Hell—but Heavenless misery—
　And bitter torments only known
　To him who loves—but lives alone !

SONG FROM THE INNER LIFE.

I.

Sing to the Lord, oh! weary soul of sorrow!
 Sing to the Lord, though chastened by his rod!
Sing to the Lord that others hope may borrow—
   "The pure in heart see God."

II.

Sink not beneath the yoke of tribulation,
 Poor weary mortal on life's thorny road!
But bear up stately with this consolation—
   "The pure in heart see God."

III.

Take up thy Cross—when thou art weary laden,
 Think how Christ sank beneath the heavy load!
High over Calvary shines the Heavenly Aiden—
   "The pure in heart see God."

IV.

Cherish the Golden Words that he has spoken,
 Then march up Calvary with thy heavy load,
Where his pure body on the Cross was broken—
   "The pure in heart see God."

V.

His yoke is easy—light, too, is his burden—
Death is the Gate to his Divine Abode—
The Land of Promise lies beyond the Jordan—
" The pure in heart see God."

VI.

Angels of Light their vigils now are keeping,
Crowding the ladder up to Heaven's Abode—
While Jacob soft on Bethel-Plain lies sleeping—
" The pure in heart see God."

VII.

A flood of glory down from Heaven comes streaming,
Washing the Angels white along the road—
While, weary with his wrestling, he lies dreaming—
" The pure in heart see God."

VIII.

God's golden glory up the East is springing,
Flooding with splendor all that Blest Abode,
While Angels cluster at the High Gates singing—
" The pure in heart see God."

IX.

Rising, re-strengthened, like the Blest Immortals
Climbing the ladder, from the dewy sod,
He hears again at Heaven's crystalline portals—
" The pure in heart see God."

X.

Thus, while the good are on the dark earth sleeping,
  Weary with travelling on life's thorny road—
Angels around their heads strict watch are keeping—
          " The pure in heart see God."

XI.

So, while the thorns are round the good man springing,
  Bleeding his feet till they baptize the sod—
Angels of Light are to his high soul singing—
          " The pure in heart see God."

XII.

Wide as Ezekiel's ever-flowing river,
  No eye could see across it was so broad—
Shall this sweet song flow down the world forever—
          " The pure in heart see God."

THE FALLEN TEMPLE.

~~~~~~~~~~~~~

"The man of God lives longer without a tomb than any by one, invisibly interred
by angels."—*Sir Thomas Brown.*

—

I.

The body of this man is dead!
Once there was wisdom in his head;
Soon he will in the grave be laid—
His soul in immortality arrayed.

II.

For in his body—God-loved One!
It dwelt as light does in the sun;
But now his Week of Life is done—
The Sabbath of sweet rest begun.

III.

In Death's great whirlwind he did hear
God's voice upon his listening ear
Breaking in accents silver-clear—
" The Goal that thou dost seek is near."

IV.

His soul with wisdom was replete;
He walked with Hell beneath his feet;
The music that he made was sweet;
Beside God's throne he takes his seat.

V.

God's splendor round his head did glow,
Because his heart did overflow
With pity for another's woe—
Such goodness God alone could know.

VI.

His heart replied unto his head—
With wisdom it was always fed;
One to the other ministered—
For what one felt the other said.

VII.

His Angel-soul was made to be
A Green Isle in God's Silver Sea,
Whose thoughts were Flowers of Poetry,
Blooming therein eternally.

VIII.

Such prospect did his soul command,
From this dark world, where he did stand,
He saw in Heaven the Promised Land—
Beyond the starry shining band.

IX.

Then did his giant soul give birth
To this great thought in going forth—
*The greatest, God-like thing on earth
Is homage done to human worth.*

x.

Prophetic music did he make
For his own soul's eternal sake,
When Death did all his heart-strings break—
Then from life's death did he awake.

xi.

With intellectual travail throes
Did he give birth to those great woes
Which no one but the Poet knows—
And, knowing, knoweth no repose.

THE LILY OF HEAVEN.

I.

Now in her snow-white shroud she lies—
(Her lily lids half veil her eyes)—
As if she looked with wild surprise
Up at her soul in Paradise.

II.

Her hands lie folded on her breast—
Crossed like the Cross that gave her rest;
She looks as if some heavenly guest
Had told her that her soul was blest.

III.

She lies as if she seemed to hear
Sphere-music breaking on her ear—
Breaking in accents silver-clear—
In concert with her soul up there.

IV.

Her body was the Temple bright
In which her soul dwelt full of light,
Triumphing over Death's dark night—
High Heaven laid open to the sight.

V.

Burning with pure seraphic love,
Veiled in the meekness of the dove—
Her soul, now all things past to prove,
Looks down on me from Heaven above.

VI.

For her Religion grew more bright,
The darker grew the world's dark night—
Filling her soul with such pure light,
High heaven seemed opened to her sight.

VII.

The calmness of divinest ease
Rests on her brow—upon her face—
Expressive of her soul's release
From this dark world to one of peace.

VIII.

Her pale, cold, silent lips, comprest,
Speak out to me, most manifest,
A silent language, of the rest
That she now feels among the blest.

IX.

I wept warm tears upon her face,
As she lay there in Death's embrace;
Whereon no passion could we trace—
But calmness—meekness—heavenly grace.

X.

With saintly, pale-face thus she went
Out of this world's great discontent,
Up through the starry firmament,
Into the Place of Pure Content.

CATHOLIC HYMN TO THE VIRGIN.

I.

Santa Maria! hear! oh! hear!
And turn to me thy gracious ear;
For thou art to the sorrowing near,
And, to the Catholic ever dear!

II.

Like some clear fountain, deep as strong,
My soul doth pour out, all night long,
Deep gushes of ecstatic song,
Begging thee to forgive my wrong!

III.

Thy Son, dear Mary! though on high,
Is to the needy ever nigh—
Ready to help them when they sigh—
He will not suffer me to die!

IV.

Speak not, dear Mary! for he hears
My bitter cries—beholds my tears!
Soon he will banish all my fears,
And give me strength for future years.

V.

Reach down thy lily hand so white,
And lift me up from this dark night,
To where thy Son, in glory bright,
Sits now arrayed in robes of light.

VI.

For how my soul doth long to go
Out of this world of suffering so—
Suffering as he did here below—
Thy Son alone in Heaven dost know !

VII.

For those that were most dear to me
Are gone now to eternity—
Living in Angel-purity,
Star-crowned, around God's throne with thee !

VIII.

A respite from this trying pain
My soul now seeks in song again—
Wasting away my heart to gain
Thy blissful love—but not in vain.

IX.

I think I hear thy soft replies
Dawning upon me from the skies—
Wiping the heart-dew from mine eyes,
Till all my grief within me dies.

X.

My soul, now purified by thought,
Into thy blissful arms is caught,

Whose presence, like thy Son's, when sought,
Comes when we most expect it not.

XI.

Such rapture now my heart doth swell
As nothing earthly can excel—
Lifting me up from this dark Hell
To Heaven above with thee to dwell.

XII.

The bloody sweat oozed from the brow
Of thy dear Son on earth below !
And how my soul doth love him now,
That Son alone in Heaven dost know.

SONG OF LE VERRIER

ON DISCOVERING A NEW PLANET.

I.

Circling the Cyclic-chorus of the spheres,
    Sphering the Epicycle of his song—
He sings his anthems, through th' eternal years,
    Outside the orb-paths of th' Empyreal throng.

II.

Floating in chariot of celestial fire,
    Sphered Heavenward through th' Empyreal Ether-Sea,
He rays his sphere-tones out unto the choir
    Of God until they fill Eternity.

III.

Tempestuous whirlwinds of deep melody
    Dash from his orb-prow on his spheric road—
Rolling in mountain-billows on Heaven's sea
    Against the white shore of the feet of God.

IV.

Shouting Excelsior to the starry choir
    Flooded with rapture, now he Heavenward rolls,
Glinting those golden tones of lightning-fire
    Proceeding swiftly from the Angels' souls.

SONNET.

THE RELEASE OF FIONNUALA.*

Beside an island in an inland sea,
A virgin Swan came, in the time of spring,
Her Heaven-revealing, dying song to sing!
Veiled in the night's divine tranquillity,
Far in the reeds, where she had come to float,
There rose up from her silver-sounding throat
A whirlwind of cherubic melody,
Which hurricaned the silence of the night,
And rapt with an immortal ecstacy—
(Making them think it day in their delight)—
The birds within the solitudes—when right
To Heaven, transfigured, glorified, she went,
Leaving the world in mute astonishment—
Drowned in the deluge of her agony.

---

* "Fionnuala, the daughter of Lir, was, by some supernatural power,
transformed into a swan, and condemned to wander, for many hundred
years, over certain lakes and rivers in Ireland, till the coming of Christi-
anity, when the sound of the first mass-bell was to be the signal of
her release."

SHILOH.

"He came as far as to the ANCIENT of days."—*Literal Version.*

I.

The Gospel he came down to preach,
No other one had power to teach ;
The highest Angel failed to reach
The music that was in his speech.

II.

Out of his soul's great sea did flow
Rivers of truth for man to know ;
Which, unto those who saw them so,
Made Heaven come down on earth below

III.

Those world-old Truths that lay concealed
In God's great heart—(to him revealed)
Like some great fountain, just unsealed,
Out of his soul in thunder pealed.

IV.

Great Messenger of Heavenly Truth
(Perpetual pulchritude his youth)
Sent down from Heaven with God-like ruth
To sing the barren rough world smoothe.

V.

His God-like voice made dumb the choir
Of Heaven with his great Seraph-lyre,
When from his soul divine desire
Gushed forth in notes of living fire.

VI.

His sun-like soul with glory bright,
Dissolved away the world's dark night ;
Then rising up with Gabriel might,
Went back to Heaven on wings of light.

ORPHIC EVANGEL.

I.

When shall the GOLDEN WORDS that once were spoken
  By our great august Lord be heard by men ?
His beautiful body on the cross once broken,
  Be made the model of our lives again ?
      This is the burden of my song—
        " How long, Oh ! Lord ! how long ?"

II.

How long before the Gabriel Years, all golden,
  Shall walk the world where Sin has walked so long—
Crushing with God-like tread the Ages Olden
  Out of our hearts, that we may grow as strong !
      This is the burden of my song—
        " How long, Oh ! Lord ! how long ?"

III.

How long before Man's form of Angel-beauty,
  Dead in earth's tomb, where it has lain so long,
Shall rise again, redeemed, to do its duty,
  And, like Christ's Angel, die no more by wrong ?
      This is the burden of my song—
        " How long, Oh ! Lord ! how long ?"

IV.

Like the great Prophet when he stood benighted,
  Waiting to see God's SUN in glory shine ;
My faith-uplifted soul beholds, delighted,
  The far-off shining of the LIGHT DIVINE !
      This shall engage my song—
        " How long, Oh ! Lord ! how long ?"

7

TO ONE IN PARADISE

I.

Oh ! return, love ! return from that dark lonely Dwelling,
  The sad silent grave where thy beauty is laid !
To the heart that is mourning—the bosom now swelling
  To pillow thy form lying low with the dead !
  Thy beautiful form lying low with the dead !

II.

Oh ! return, that mine eyes, which are red now with weeping,
  May behold thy dear presence once Heaven to me !
And restore the dead Joys that are silently sleeping
  Beneath the damp sod in that cold grave with thee !
  The cold clammy sod in that dark grave with thee !

III.

Though they say that from death there can be no returning,
  Oh ! break the stern bars that confine thee beneath !
And recall the bright soul that in Heaven is burning
  To light back thy form from the Valley of Death !
  Thy beautiful form from the Valley of Death !

IV.

Oh ! return like the Star that in Heaven is shining—
  Return to illumine this life's dim abode !
And restore the dark soul that is silently pining
  To meet thee again in the bosom of God !
  With thy beautiful Christ in the bosom of God !

LILIES OF LOVE.

—

LA CONTADINA.

" Il vago spirito ardente
E'n alto intelletto, un puro core."—*Petrarcha.*

—

" She seemed a splendid Angel newly drest,
Save wings, for Heaven."—*Keats.*

—

Her tender Breasts were like two snow-white Doves
   Upon one willow bough at calm of even,
Telling each other, side by side, their loves
   In soft celestial tones as sweet as Heaven.
And as the soft winds, from the flowery grove,
   Sway them thus sitting on that willow-bough,
At every breath—at every sigh of love—
   They undulate upon her bosom now.

Two dove-like spirits on her eyelids knelt,
   And weighed them gently, covering half her eyes,
Whose soul in their own azure seemed to melt
   And mingle, as the sunlight with the skies.
Her eyes were like two violets bathed in dew
   In which each lash was mirrored dark within,
As in some Lake, reflecting Heaven so blue,
   The willow-bough's long languid limbs are seen.

As God's celestial look is far too bright
   For Angel's gaze in Heaven if not kept dim,
And partly shorn of its excessive light
   By the broad pinions of the cherubim ;
So, these two spirits, one on each fair lid,
   Let down the lash-fringed curtain to conceal
And keep but half that heavenly glory hid,
   Which it were death to mortals to reveal.

GOOD NIGHT.

I.

Now the Nightingale sits singing,
   By his Rose-bud in the grove,
While the Heavens above are ringing
   With his river-song of love.
Like the wild Swan on the ocean,
   Circled with her Cygnets white,
Star-engirdled, with soft motion,
    Sails the Moon through Heaven to-night.
       Good night, my Love ! my dearest !
       High heaven of my delight !
       Of all things brightest, fairest !
       My Beautiful—good night !

II.

Go—while thou art softly sleeping
   By the clear Elysian streams,
I will be awake here weeping
   By the " Ivory gate of Dreams."
Angels, like the stars in number,
   Watchers from their Courts of Light,
Sing around thy peaceful slumber
   Through the beautiful good night.
       Good night, my Love ! my dearest !
       High Heaven of my delight !
       Of all things brightest, fairest !
       My Beautiful—good night !

III.

While the odorous flowers are closing
    Their soft petals in the dew,
Thou wilt be in bed reposing—
    I awake in mine for you.
Take, oh, take to your soft bosom!
Faithful nurse of my DELIGHT!
This sweet Lily-bell in blossom,
    And preserve her there, GOOD NIGHT!
        Good night, my Love! my dearest!
        High heaven of my delight!
        Of all things brightest, fairest!
        My Beautiful—good night!

IV.

Here we both stand broken hearted,
    Leaning on each other's heart;
For in parting we seem parted,
    Just to think that we must part.
See! the pale, cold moon is waning—
    Sinking softly from our sight—
While our souls are here complaining
    For the loss of our good night!
        Good night, my Love! my dearest!
        High Heaven of my delight!
        Of all things brightest, fairest!
        My Beautiful—good night!

V.

Where the Nightingale sits singing
    By his Rose-bud in the grove,
While the Heavens above are ringing
    With his river-song of love;

While my soul is left here sighing
　　Out its song for my DELIGHT,
I now hear her voice replying
　　Unto mine, "*My Love! good night!*"
　　　　Good night, my Love! my dearest!
　　　　High Heaven of my delight!
　　　　Of all things brightest, fairest!
　　　　My Beautiful—good night!

LOVE.

I.

What is it that makes the maiden
  So like Christ in Heaven above ?
Or, like Heavenly Eve in Aiden,
  Meeting Adam, blushing :—love—
             Love, love, love !
       ECHO.
       Love !

II.

What is it that makes the murmur
  Of the plaintive turtle dove
Fill our hearts with so much Summer
  'Till they melt to passion ?—love—
             Love, love, love !
       ECHO.
       Love !

III.

See the Rose unfold her bosom
  To the amorous Sun above—
Bursting into fragrant blossom
  At his sight !—what is it ?—love—
             Love, love, love !
       ECHO.
       Love !

IV.

Like the peace-song of the Angels
  Sent to one from Heaven above
Who believes in Christ's Evangels—
  Is the voice of one in love—
                    Love, love, love!
          ECHO.
            Love!

V.

Christ, who once on earth was sorry,
  Captain of the host above,
Left his Father's throne of glory
  To redeem us by his love—
                    Love, love, love!
          ECHO.
            Love!

VI.

Why was he made Mediator—
  Stooping from the Heavens above?
Was he not our Great Creator?
  Angels answer—" God is Love"—
                    Love, love, love!
          ECHO.
            Love!

VII.

All the Christian Constellations
  Choiring through the realms above,
Soon would cease their ministrations
  Were it not for thee, oh! Love!
                    Love, love, love!
          ECHO.
            Love!

THE VOICE OF THOUGHT.

Faint as the far-down tone
  Beneath the sounding sea,
Muffled, by its own moan,
  To silent melody;
So faint we cannot tell
  But that the sound we hear
Is some sweet roses' smell
  That falls upon our ear;
(As if the Butterfly,
  Shaking the Lily-bell,
While drinking joyfully,
  Should toll its own death-knell!)
Sweeter than Hope's sweet lute
  Singing of joys to be,
When Pain's harsh voice is mute,
  Is the Soul's sweet song to me.

7*

SONG TO ISA.

I.

Upon thy lips now lies
　The music-dew of love;
And in thy deep blue eyes,
　More mild than heaven above,
　The meekness of the dove.

II.

More sweet than the perfume
　Of snow-white jessamine,
When it is first in bloom,
　Is that sweet breath of thine,
　Which mingles now with mine.

III.

Like an Æolian sound,
　Out of an ocean shell,
Which fills the air around
　With music, such as fell
　From lips of ISRAFEL;

IV.

Over thy lips now flow,
  Out of thy heart for me,
Sweet songs, which none can know
  But him who hopes to be
  Forevermore with thee.

V.

And like the snow-white Dove
  Frightened from earth at even
On tempests borne above,—
  My swift-winged soul is driven
  Upon thy voice to heaven !

EULALIE.

I.

Her rich cascade of hair,
  Around her swan-like throat,
Down on her bosom bare,
  In wavy gold doth float.

II.

Her lily-lidded eyes,
  Burning in their own light,
Seem melted from the skies,
  They are so Heavenly bright.

III.

Her hands are rosy-white,
  Like lilies in the sun ;
Her countenance makes bright
  All that she smiles upon.

IV.

Her words are soft as dew
  Dropt on some flower at even,
As if, (though known to few,)
  She spoke the tongue of Heaven.

V.

As when the summer South
  A rose-bud doth dispart,
The lips of her sweet mouth
  Seem opened by her heart.

VI.

As perfume from the rose,
    Just opening, from her tongue
The soul of fragrance flows
    Out of her heart in song.

VII.

Her breath is like the sweet
    Perfume of flowers at even,
When all the rarest meet,
    And every one is Heaven.

VIII.

As joyful hearts of birds
    High overflow in song,
Her innocent heart in words
    Flows golden from her tongue.

IX.

All things to her seem pure,
    Because her heart is so ;
Ah ! how can she endure
    The real truth to know ?

X.

Sweeter than harp or lute
    Is her sweet song to me ;
Softer than Dorian flute
    Her Lydian melody.

XI.

As Pæans of wild bliss
    The birds pour forth in Spring,
So, Heaven the Thesis is
    Of all that she doth sing

XII.

Ah! how my soul doth love
  To hear her sing at even—
Singing, on earth, above
  Sweet Israfel in Heaven.

XIII.

Mild as some breeze at noon—
  Soft as the pale cold light
Rained from the full-orbed moon
  Upon the down of night.

XIV.

For when her song doth move
  Her trembling lips apart,
The joys of Heaven above
  Seem poured into my heart.

XV.

Sweet as the fragrance smells
  Of lily-bells at even,
Is that sweet song which tells,
  On earth, the joys of Heaven

XVI.

Sweeter than voice of swan
  Upon some Summer sea,
Piling to Heaven, at dawn,
  His clarion melody.

XVII.

For when she sings at night,
  The stars appear to me
To burn more Heavenly bright
  In her sweet symphony.

XVIII.

Soft words from off the eaves
  Of her sweet lips now fall,
Like dew drops from the leaves
  Of roses—rhythmical.

XIX.

For as the rose-lipped shell
  The riches of the sea ;
So does her song now tell
  Her heart's deep love for me.

XX.

Star of my life's dark night !
  Thou wert to me first given—
Bright Vesper of delight !
  To lead my soul to Heaven.

LILY ADAIR.

I.

The Apollo Belvidere was adorning
    The Chamber where Eulalie lay,
While Aurora, the Rose of the Morning,
    Smiled full in the face of the Day.
All around stood the beautiful Graces
    Bathing Venus—some combing her hair—
While she lay in her husband's embraces*
    A-moulding my LILY ADAIR—
    Of my Fawn-like LILY ADAIR—
    Of my Dove-like LILY ADAIR—
    Of my beautiful, dutiful LILY ADAIR.

II.

Where the Oreads played in the Highlands,
    And the Water-Nymphs bathed in the streams,
In the tall Jasper Reeds of the Islands—
    She wandered in life's early dreams.
For the Wood-Nymphs then brought from the Wildwood
    The turtle Doves Venus kept there,
Which the Dryades tamed, in his childhood,

---

* It was a beautiful Idea of the Greeks that the procreation of beau-
tiful children might be promoted by keeping in their sleeping apart-
ments an Apollo or Hyacinthus. In this way they not only patronized
Art, but begat a likeness of their own love.

For Cupid, to LILY ADAIR—
To my Dove-like LILY ADAIR—
To my lamb-like LILY ADAIR—
To my beautiful, dutiful LILY ADAIR.

III.

Where the Opaline Swan circled, singing,
  With her eider-down Cygnets at noon,
In the tall Jasper Reeds that were springing
  From the marge of the crystal Lagoon—
Rich Canticles, clarion-like, golden,
  Such as only true love can declare,
Like an Archangel's voice in times olden—
  I went with my LILY ADAIR—
  With my lamb-like LILY ADAIR—
  With my saint-like LILY ADAIR—
  With my beautiful, dutiful LILY ADAIR.

IV.

Her eyes, lily-lidded, were azure,
  Cerulian, celestial, divine—
Suffused with the soul-light of pleasure,
  Which drew all the soul out of mine.
She had all the rich grace of the Graces,
  And all that they had not to spare;
For it took all their beautiful faces
  To make one for LILY ADAIR—
  For my Christ-like LILY ADAIR—
  For my Heaven-born LILY ADAIR—
  For my beautiful, dutiful LILY ADAIR.

V.

She was fairer by far than that Maiden,
  The star-bright Cassiope,
Who was taken by Angels to Aiden,
  And crowned with eternity.

For her beauty the Sea-Nymphs offended,
  Because so surpassingly fair;
And so death then the precious life ended
  Of my beautiful LILY ADAIR—
  Of my Heaven-born LILY ADAIR—
  Of my star-crowned LILY ADAIR—
  Of my beautiful, dutiful LILY ADAIR.

VI.

From her Paradise-Isles in the ocean,
  To the beautiful City of On,
By the mellifluent rivers of Goshen,
  My beautiful Lily is gone!
In her Chariot of Fire translated,
  Like Elijah, she passed through the air,
To the City of God golden-gated—
  The Home of my LILY ADAIR—
  Of my star-crowned LILY ADAIR—
  Of my God-loved LILY ADAIR—
  Of my beautiful, dutiful LILY ADAIR.

VII.

On the vista-path made by the Angels,
  In her Chariot of Fire, she rode,
While the Cherubim sang their Evangels—
  To the Gates of the City of God.
For the Cherubim-band that went with her,
  I saw them pass out of the air—
I saw them go up through the ether
  Into Heaven with my LILY ADAIR—
  With my Christ-like LILY ADAIR—
  With my God-loved LILY ADAIR—
  With my beautiful, dutiful LILY ADAIR.

SONNET.

ON READING MILTON'S PARADISE LOST

Sweet as that soul-uplifting Hydromel
  Idean Ganymede did give to Jove
  In the God-kingdoms of Immortal Love—
Dipt from Heaven's everlasting Golden Well—
Was thy great song, celestial ISRAFEL!
    Like that Apollo near the shining portals
  Of Heaven, in chariot, with celestial lyre,
    Sung for the thronging glorified Immortals,
  Which set the souls of all the gods on fire !
So sweet my soul, entranced, seemed suddenly brought
  Before the star-crowned, blazing majesty
Of those great Sages of immortal thought,
  And Poet-kings of deathless melody,
    Who now shake Heaven with thunderous Jubilee.

THE QUEEN OF LOVE.

LA REINETTE DE MON CŒUR.

A bright enameled Brooch of purest gold
  She sported in her sunny-silken hair;
New lilac satin did her limbs enfold,
  While round her Moon-like brow more fair
Than Heaven when all the sky is clear,
  A Diamond-studded chain of gold she wore,
Starred in the centre with her feronnier
  Which shone like Vesper on the heavenly shore.

A glove of spotless kid enclosed her hand;
  A golden Bracelet circled each fair wrist;
The ground on which her tender feet did stand
  Was by her Kid-ensandaled feet imprest,
Like letters written by an Angel's hand
In Hieroglyphics of the Heavenly Land:
  And all who saw her said she was possest
  Of beauty that would make an Angel blest.

An Antique Cameo starred her silver vest,
  Fit emblem of her heart it did unfold—
Couched in the valley of her snow-white breast,
  Encased in circles of the purest gold.
The rich Design which graced the Gem was this;
  A snow-white Dove, perched on a Tulip-Vase,
Was sipping nectar from the Chalice full,
  While by her side there stood, with artless grace,
Her mate, drinking, in Art most beautiful—
  This Antique Symbol set there to express,
  In loftiest Art, her artful artlessness.

The Romantic Tradition in American Literature

An Arno Press Collection

Alcott, A. Bronson, editor. **Conversations with Children on the Gospels.** Boston, 1836/1837. Two volumes in one.

Bartol, C[yrus] A. **Discourses on the Christian Spirit and Life.** 2nd edition. Boston, 1850.

Boker, George H[enry]. **Poems of the War.** Boston, 1864.

Brooks, Charles T. **Poems, Original and Translated.** Selected and edited by W. P. Andrews. Boston, 1885.

Brownell, Henry Howard. **War-Lyrics** and Other Poems. Boston, 1866.

Brownson, O[restes] A. **Essays and Reviews Chiefly on Theology, Politics, and Socialism.** New York, 1852.

Channing, [William] Ellery (The Younger). **Poems.** Boston, 1843.

Channing, [William] Ellery (The Younger). **Poems of Sixty-Five Years.** Edited by F. B. Sanborn. Philadelphia and Concord, 1902.

Chivers, Thomas Holley. **Eonchs of Ruby:** A Gift of Love. New York, 1851.

Chivers, Thomas Holley. **Virginalia;** or, Songs of My Summer Nights. (Reprinted from *Research Classics,* No. 2, 1942). Philadelphia, 1853.

Cooke, Philip Pendleton. **Froissart Ballads,** and Other Poems. Philadelphia, 1847.

Cranch, Christopher Pearse. **The Bird and the Bell,** with Other Poems. Boston, 1875.

[Dall], Caroline W. Healey, editor. **Margaret and Her Friends.** Boston, 1895.

[D'Arusmont], Frances Wright. **A Few Days in Athens.** Boston, 1850.

Everett, Edward. **Orations and Speeches,** on Various Occasions. Boston, 1836.

Holland, J[osiah] G[ilbert]. **The Marble Prophecy,** and Other Poems. New York, 1872.

Huntington, William Reed. **Sonnets and a Dream.** Jamaica, N. Y., 1899.

Jackson, Helen [Hunt]. **Poems.** Boston, 1892.

Miller, Joaquin (Cincinnatus Hiner Miller). **The Complete Poetical Works of Joaquin Miller.** San Francisco, 1897.

Parker, Theodore. **A Discourse of Matters Pertaining to Religion.** Boston, 1842.

Pinkney, Edward C. **Poems.** Baltimore, 1838.

Reed, Sampson. **Observations on the Growth of the Mind.** *Including,* **Genius** (Reprinted from *Aesthetic Papers,* Boston, 1849). 5th edition. Boston, 1859.

Sill, Edward Rowland. **The Poetical Works of Edward Rowland Sill.** Boston and New York, 1906.

Simms, William Gilmore. **Poems:** Descriptive, Dramatic, Legendary and Contemplative. New York, 1853. Two volumes in one.

Simms, William Gilmore, editor. **War Poetry of the South.** New York, 1866.

Stickney, Trumbull. **The Poems of Trumbull Stickney.** Boston and New York, 1905.

Timrod, Henry. **The Poems of Henry Timrod.** Edited by Paul H. Hayne. New York, 1873.

Trowbridge, John Townsend. **The Poetical Works of John Townsend Trowbridge.** Boston and New York, 1903.

Very, Jones. **Essays and Poems.** [Edited by R. W. Emerson]. Boston, 1839.

Very, Jones. **Poems and Essays.** Boston and New York, 1886.

White, Richard Grant, editor. **Poetry:** Lyrical, Narrative, and Satirical of the Civil War. New York, 1866.

Wilde, Richard Henry. **Hesperia:** A Poem. Edited by His Son (William Wilde). Boston, 1867.

Willis, Nathaniel Parker. **The Poems, Sacred, Passionate, and Humorous, of Nathaniel Parker Willis.** New York, 1868.